Statistics
and
Measurement
in the Classroom

Cover design by Mauricio Charpenel. The
Diego Rivera drawing is reprinted from
An Artist Grows Up in Mexico by Leah
Brenner with permission of the author.

PSYCHOLOGICAL FOUNDATIONS OF EDUCATION SERIES

THE TEACHER AS A PERSON

Luiz F. S. Natalicio
Carl F. Hereford
Guy N. Martin

UNDERSTANDING STUDENTS' BEHAVIOR

Carl F. Hereford
Luiz F. S. Natalicio
Michal Clark

STATISTICS AND MEASUREMENT IN THE CLASSROOM

Carl F. Hereford
Luiz F. S. Natalicio
Susan J. McFarland

Statistics
and
Measurement
in the Classroom

•

Edited by

Susan J. McFarland
Carl F. Hereford

Department of Educational Psychology
The University of Texas at Austin

Second Edition

wcb

WM. C. BROWN COMPANY PUBLISHERS
Dubuque, Iowa

Printed in the United States of America

Contents

Preface

Why Should Teachers Study Statistics? To those of you who are saying, "Now, that's a good question," we say that it is one you have every right to ask. It is also one which we are obliged to answer.

Teachers need to understand basic statistical concepts because:

1. Simple descriptive statistical ideas can help in assessing the performance of your classes and the effectiveness of your teaching in a way which is more accurate than guesses or hunches.

2. As standardized psychological tests are used more and more for placement and assessment in school systems, it becomes necessary for teachers to have some understanding of what scores on these instruments do and do not mean. Since the construction and scoring procedures for such tests rest on statistical foundations, their appropriate use and interpretation necessitate knowledge of basic statistical concepts.

3. Education today is no longer a static institution. Innovative research is constantly being done, and such research is typically reported in educational and psychological journals. This information is important to teachers, and such journals cannot be understood without a degree of familiarity with statistical terms and concepts.

In addition, the statistical conclusions and data reported in standardized test manuals and research journals are not sacred just because they are quantitative. Any statistical statement or test score should be approached with a healthy measure of educated skepticism The information can then be used for what it is worth. The validity of all such results is entirely dependent on the worth of the basic data and the appropriateness of the operations performed. Statistics must be understood in its proper perspective as a very useful means—but never an end in itself.

* * *

Convinced? Probably not, for there is always the familiar story which begins with a dislike of math and ends with the notion that since statistics is based on math, it must be equally disagreeable. But statistics involves a great deal more than its mathematical foundation—ideas, applications, ways of looking at things. When approached as a mass of formulas, derivations and definitions, statistics should indeed remain the province of the mathematician and the researcher. When approached conceptually, however, basic statistics takes on relevance for anyone who deals with other people in a way that involves evaluation. The student-teacher relationship involves much more than evaluation, as indicated by the content of the other two volumes in this series. Evaluation, however, remains an integral part of the teacher's role—despite his personal feelings on the subject. Anyone who evaluates others operates on statistical notions whether he is aware of it or not. He makes certain explicit or implicit assumptions about individual differences, average performance, the relationship of one type of behavior to others, and the meaning of grades. It is inevitable that evaluative behavior in teachers will be based on many such assumptions—made by each individual teacher about the distribution of his students in a personal statistical world.

This is not an exercise in drudgery. It is an opportunity for you to become aware of your own assumptions about human variability and performance—to clarify and make more accurate your own statistical framework. Like it or not, you will someday fit your students into it.

Why Should Teachers Study Statistics?

To those of you who are saying, "Now, that's a good question," we say that it is one you have every right to ask. It is also one which we are obliged to answer.

Teachers need to understand basic statistical concepts because:

1. Simple descriptive statistical ideas can help in assessing the performance of your classes and the effectiveness of your teaching in a way which is more accurate than guesses or hunches.

2. As standardized psychological tests are used more and more for placement and assessment in school systems, it becomes necessary for teachers to have some understanding of what scores on these instruments do and do not mean. Since the construction and scoring procedures for such tests rest on statistical foundations, their appropriate use and interpretation necessitate knowledge of basic statistical concepts.

3. Education today is no longer a static institution. Innovative research is constantly being done, and such research is typically reported in educational and psychological journals. This information is important to teachers, and such journals cannot be understood without a degree of familiarity with statistical terms and concepts.

In addition, the statistical conclusions and data reported in standardized test manuals and research journals are not sacred just because they are quantitative. Any statistical statement or test score should be approached with a healthy measure of educated skepticism. The information can then be used for what it is worth. The validity of all such results is entirely dependent on the worth of the basic data and the appropriateness of the operations performed. Statistics must be understood in its proper perspective as a very useful means—but never an end in itself.

* * *

Convinced? Probably not, for there is always the familiar story which begins with a dislike of math and ends with the notion that since statistics is based on math, it must be equally disagreeable. But statistics involves a great deal more than its mathematical foundation—ideas, applications, ways of looking at things. When approached as a mass of formulas, derivations and definitions, statistics should indeed remain the province of the mathematician and the researcher. When approached conceptually, however, basic statistics takes on relevance for anyone who deals with other people in a way that involves evaluation. The student-teacher relationship involves much more than evaluation, as indicated by the content of the other two volumes in this series. Evaluation, however, remains an integral part of the teacher's role—despite his personal feelings on the subject. Anyone who evaluates others operates on statistical notions whether he is aware of it or not. He makes certain explicit or implicit assumptions about individual differences, average performance, the relationship of one type of behavior to others, and the meaning of grades. It is inevitable that evaluative behavior in teachers will be based on many such assumptions—made by each individual teacher about the distribution of his students in a personal statistical world.

This is not an exercise in drudgery. It is an opportunity for you to become aware of your own assumptions about human variability and performance—to clarify and make more accurate your own statistical framework. Like it or not, you will someday fit your students into it.

I: Basic Statistical Concepts

1. Statistical Terms and Statements

Allen L. Edwards

Averages

In our daily conversation, we often use the term "average." We say that "John is better than average" when someone questions us about his golfing ability, or that "Mary is an average student and slightly below average in height." Some of our college courses we say we like "better than average." Some of our instructors are described as "average teachers." And, although we may not have defined the term in our own thinking as precisely as a statistician would, we have some general understanding of the concept of "average." We may be vaguely aware that our statements concerning averages are based upon a series of observations or measurements, and that each of these observations, taken singly, may not be the same as the average we have in mind. We perhaps have some scale in mind when we refer to John's ability as a golfer or Mary's height, and our average represents some middle position or value. The statement that "John is better than average" or that "Mary is slightly below average" indicates that we do not think of them in this middle position.

We can find statements similar to these in books about psychology and education. There we can find statements about the average intelligence quotient (or IQ) of a group of children, the average score made by students on a reading test, the average number of errors made by rats in learning a maze, the average number of students per teacher in a given school, the average number of hours devoted to noninstructional activities by teachers in the same school, and so on. These statements about averages, however, would be expressed more precisely than the statements we make about averages in our daily conversation. In our books and journals, averages are expressed in numbers, and the manner in which the numbers are obtained involves an elementary application of statistical methods.

Variability

A teacher recognizes the fact that, in her classes, not all students do equally well. On a test given to one class, some students may have very high scores, and others may have very low scores. The same test given to another class may result in scores that are all very similar to one another. We would say that the students in the first class are more variable in their performance than those in the second. The psychologist finds that some rats learn to run a maze with very few trials, and other rats require a large number of trials. Rats vary in their maze-learning abilities.

We constantly experience variability in daily life. We note variability in the teaching effectiveness of different teachers. We observe variability in the temperature from hour to hour, from day to day, and from month to month. We easily recognize the fact that some individuals are quite tall and others quite short. We find that some texts are relatively easy to read, and others are difficult. Textbooks differ or vary in their readability.

Statements about variability, like statements about averages, can be expressed precisely in the form of numbers. To measure the variability, sometimes called the dispersion, of a set of measurements also involves an application of elementary statistics.

Relationships

We make frequent reference to relationships in daily life, although these statements, like those we make about averages and variability, are not expressed precisely. We note that the amount of rainfall appears to be related to the season of the year, or that an individual's opinion on desegregation may be related to the section of the country in which he lives. We may say that John's golf game will improve with practice. In this instance, we indicate that we believe there is some relationship between amount of practice and performance on the golf course. The teacher observes that the scores students make on the first examination given in a course appear to be related to the scores they make on subsequent examinations.

If you will examine the textbook you used in introductory psychology, you will find many statements about relationships. Again, these statements are expressed precisely by means of numbers, and the method by which such numbers are obtained involves the application of elementary statistical methods.

Functions of Statistical Methods

Precise Description

One of the chief functions of statistical methods, as we have indicated, is to enable us to make precise statements about averages, variability, and relationships. With statistical methods, we do not have to rely upon vague impressions about these things; we can describe them accurately.

Prediction

Suppose that we had studied a group of workmen operating a particular machine, and that we had then constructed a test of some sort which we believed to be related to performance on the machine itself. Giving the test to a large number of workers, we then find, by statistical methods, that the score on the test is related to performance on the machine. Could we then predict from the scores of a *new* group of workmen how well they would probably perform on the machine in question? If we find that there is a relationship between scores on a scholastic aptitude test and grades in college for one group of students, can we use this information to predict the grades that an entering class of freshmen will make, knowing only their scholastic-aptitude-test scores and prior to their actually taking any college courses?

Statistical methods are also used in making predictions. Having made predictions, statistical methods then enable us to evaluate the accuracy and efficiency of the predictions. The problem of making predictions and evaluating predictions is also an important function of statistical methods.

Statistical Inference

Having made a series of observations and having described these particular observations in terms, let us say, of an average and a measure of variability, statistical methods, under certain conditions, enable us to take another step. Often, for example, our interest is not so much in the particular set of observations we have made, but rather in the larger supply or potential set of observations we could make, but have not. Suppose, for example, there are 12,000 students in attendance at a given school. We have given a test to 400 of the students, and for this group we have obtained a measure of their average performance and of the variability of their scores on the test. We call the particular 400 observations we have made a *sample*. The complete set of 12,000 potential observations we could make we call a *population*. If we obtain a descriptive measure for the sample, such as an average or measure of variability, we call this measure a *statistic*. The corresponding measure for the population is called a *parameter*.

An important function of statistical methods is the problem of estimating population parameters from sample statistics, and the function is referred to as one of estimation. The process by which we arrive at such estimations is known as *statistical inference*. By this process we can generalize, under specified conditions, from knowledge of a characteristic of a sample to a characteristic of the population. In the case described above, for example, let us assume that the sample is representative of the population. We may wish to use our knowledge of the average and variability of the 400 sample observations as a basis for generalizing about the corresponding measures or parameters for the population of 12,000 observations. Since such generalizations are always subject to error, it is important to have some measure of the degree of confidence we have in making the generalization. The manner in which we do this is to specify limits within which we are confident that a parameter falls. These limits are called *confidence limits*. The degree of confidence associated with these limits is called a *confidence coefficient*.

Another problem in statistical inference concerns whether or not it is reasonable to conclude that two or more averages, or other measures, differ significantly. In experimental work, for example, we may measure the performance of two groups of subjects, each under a different experimental condition. If the average performance of the two groups of subjects under the two experimental conditions is not the same, this may be the result of chance factors, rather than any difference in the experimental conditions themselves. Can we conclude that the difference in the average performance under the two experimental conditions is of such magnitude that it cannot reasonably be attributed to chance? If so, we say that the difference is significant. Statistical inference provides us with tests that can be used in judging the significance of differences. These tests are appropriately called *tests of significance.*

2. Variables and Scales

Allen L. Edwards

The fundamental importance of observing things is recognized by all sciences. Those things that scientists observe are frequently called variates or *variables*. For example, if the thing we are observing is the intelligence quotient (IQ) of children, our variable is the IQ. Any particular observation is a *value of the variable*. In our example, an observation of the particular IQ associated with a particular child is a value of the variable. The value of the variable indicates the *class* to which an observation is assigned. If the value of the variable is 100, we consider that observation and all others with a value of 100 as belonging to the same class. Obviously, if something is to be designated as a variable, we must have at least two possible classes of observations. These classes must also be mutually exclusive; that is, any particular observation can be assigned to only one of the available classes. By a variable, therefore, we mean anything that we can observe in such a way that our observations can be classified into one of any number of mutually exclusive classes.

Psychological Variables

In the behavioral sciences, one general class of variables we are concerned with is that relating to the behavior of organisms. By behavior, we mean any action

---

of an organism. In some cases, the behavior we observe may be a relatively simple response, and in other cases a quite complex pattern of responses. The bar-pressing behavior of a rat in a Skinner box, for example, would be considered a relatively simple variable compared with the aggressive behavior of a client in therapy or the withdrawal reactions of a child in nursery school. The general class of things we observe relating to behavior we call *behavioral variables.*

Behavior, however, is not the only thing that a behavioral scientist observes. We have referred to the behavior of a rat *in* a Skinner box, the behavior of a client *in* therapy, the actions of a child *in* a nursery school. Behavior always occurs in a particular setting or environment, and with respect to certain conditions of stimulation present in the environment. Our interest in the environment is based upon the assumption that behavior in a particular setting is, in some degree, a response to that setting and the conditions of stimulation which it provides. The general class of things we observe that relate to the environment, situation, or conditions of stimulation, we may designate as *stimulus variables.*

There is still another general class of things that we observe, and these things relate to properties or characteristics of organisms. We shall call this general class of variables *organismic variables.* For example, the thing we observe may be the color of hair associated with each of a number of individuals. Hair color would be an organismic variable, and the specific hair color of a given individual would be an observation or value of the variable. Similarly, we might observe the heights and weights of a group of individuals. In this instance also, we would refer to height and weight as organismic variables.

As a matter of convenience, we frequently make use of *response-inferred* organismic variables. IQ's, for example, are based on observations of the behavior or responses of individuals in a standardized testing situation. We may choose, in a particular research problem, however, to regard the IQ as something that is associated with the organism and thus refer to it as an organismic variable, even though the IQ is based on observations of behavior. As another example, in a given experiment, we may select one group of subjects with high scores on the Taylor Manifest Anxiety Scale and another group with low scores on the same scale. The performance or behavior of these two groups may then be studied under certain experimental or stimulus conditions. We may find it convenient to refer to the first group as the "anxious" group and the second group as the "nonanxious" group, that is, to treat anxiety, in this instance, as an organismic variable rather than a response variable.

Scales of Measurement

Nominal Scales

Suppose that the thing we observe is the sex of an organism. Only 2 values of this variable are possible: We designate each organism as a male or a female. Our basic data thus consist of the number of observations in each of the two classes, male and female. When we have ordered variables, which we shall discuss later, the various classes of our observations can be logically arranged, say, from left to right, so that we can say that any class falling to the left of a given class has less of the variable, and any class falling to the right of a given class has more of the variable. Note that, in the case under discussion, the values of the variable are in no way ordered. If any observation is assigned the value male, this does not indicate that it has a greater or lesser degree of the variable we have called sex than an observation assigned the value female.

Observations of unordered variables, such as sex, are one of the most primitive forms of measurement and are described as constituting a *nominal scale*. In nominal scales, numbers may be substituted for the names of the various classes of the variable. The numbers serve only to identify the classes and do not indicate anything about the classes other than that they are different. The difference between the classes is one of kind and not degree. Thus we might identify all of the observations labeled male with the number 0 and all of the observations labeled female with the number 1. Since the numbers serve only to identify the classes, it would not matter if the males were identified by the number 1 and the females by the number 0. Other examples of variables in which the observations constitute a nominal scale would be individuals classified according to psychiatric diagnosis, objects classified according to color, individuals classified by state of residence, students classified according to whether they are members or nonmembers of fraternities, and so forth.

The data resulting from nominal scales are often referred to as *categorical data, frequency data, attribute data,* or *enumeration data.* The basic thing we have to deal with in such data is a count, or the number of observations in each of the classes or categories.

Ordinal Scales

In some cases, the observations we make may be ordered in such a way that we can say one observation represents more of a given variable than another observation. For example, we might take five individuals and line them up against a wall. By comparing the individuals to one another, we may be able to arrange them in order from what we judge to be the tallest to the shortest. If we identify our observations by assigning the number 5 to the tallest, 4 to the next, 3 to the next, 2 to the next, and 1 to the shortest, our observations would be described as constituting an *ordinal scale.* The numbers used in identifying our observations are called *ranks.* Ranks tell us something about the degree of the variable within the set of observations at hand. The observation with Rank 5, for example, we believe represents a greater degree of the variable than any of the other observations in the set of 5 observations.

It is important to note that, although we believe ranks tell us whether one observation represents more or less of the variable of interest than another, they do not tell us *how much* more or less. For example, we know nothing about the exact difference in degree between any two ranks. The observation assigned Rank 5 may be, in measured units, 68 inches, that assigned Rank 4 may be 66 inches, and that assigned Rank 3 may be 60 inches. From the ranks alone, we know only that we believe the observation with Rank 5 is greater than that with Rank 4, and that with Rank 4 it is greater than Rank 3, but we do not know how much greater.

Interval Scales

When the numbers used to identify observations represent not only an ordering of the observations but also convey meaningful information with respect to the distance or degree of difference between all observations, the observations are said to constitute an *interval scale*. Thus, if we have an interval scale, the numbers 7, 5, and 2, which identify 3 different observations, tell us that 7 is 2 units greater than 5 and that 5 is 3 units greater than 2; that is, the difference between 7 and 5 is 2 units, and the difference between 5 and 2 is 3 units. The difference between 7 and 2 is the sum of the difference between 7 and 5 and the difference between 5 and 2, or 2 + 3 = 5 units.

The ratio between the two intervals, 7 − 5 = 2 and 5 − 2 = 3, is 2/3. With an interval scale, we can add any number to each of the values we have or subtract any number from each of the values and still maintain the essential properties of the scale. The reason for this is that our *origin*, the value we choose to call zero, is arbitrary. Subtracting 2 from each of the three values, 7, 5, and 2, we have 5, 3, and 0, and we have arbitrarily moved our origin to the value previously designated as 2. The ratio between the two intervals, 5 − 3 = 2 and 3 − 0 = 3, is still 2/3.

Our unit of measurement for interval scales is also arbitrary. If we consider the unit of measurement for our three values, 7, 5, and 2, to be 1, then we can double the unit of measurement by multiplying each value by 2 to obtain 14, 10, and 4 as our new values. Again we may note that the ratio between the intervals, 14 − 10 = 4 and 10 − 4 = 6, is 4/6 or 2/3, the same ratio we had before.

By adding or subtracting a given number from each value of our variable and by multiplying or dividing each value of the variable by a given number, we obtain what is called a *linear transformation* of the values on an interval scale. The essential properties of an interval scale remain unchanged by any linear transformation. Adding a specified number to or subtracting a specified number from each value merely shifts the origin of the scale. Multiplication or division of each value by a specified number merely changes the unit of measurement.

With interval scales, it is not appropriate to take ratios of any two values on the scale. If we do, we change the properties of the scale. Ratios can be taken only with respect to the intervals or distances between two values. We cannot, for example, with an interval scale, say that a value of 50 is twice as great as a value of 25. This is because, as we have pointed out above, our origin on such scales is arbitrary. Suppose, for example, we can assume that scores on a vocabulary test constitute an interval scale. The score consists of the number of correct responses given to the items in the test, and we further assume that the score is a measure of a variable we choose to call vocabulary. We have three values of the variable, let us say, corresponding to scores of 25, 50, and 75. We cannot conclude that the score of 50 represents *twice* the degree of the variable as the score of 25 nor that a score of 75 represents *three* times as great a vocabulary as one of 25. For, assume that we added 25 very easy items to our test so that no one of our three subjects failed to give the correct response to them. The previous three values of our variable would now become, with our new test, 50, 75, and 100, respectively. If we falsely believed that we could form ratios between values on our interval scale, we would now falsely assume that the person with a score of 100 had *twice* as great a vocabulary as the person with a score of 50, whereas, previously, the corresponding scores of 75 and 25 would have falsely led us to believe that the one person had *three* times as great a vocabulary as the other.

Ratio Scales

The only scale on which ratios can be formed between values of a variable is one in which we have an interval scale with an *absolute zero*. Such a scale is called a *ratio scale*. Length, as measured in units of inches or feet, is a ratio scale, for the origin on this scale is an absolute zero corresponding to no length at all. Thus it is appropriate to state that an object which is 4 feet long is *twice* as long as an object that measures only 2 feet.

In ratio scales, only the unit of measurement is arbitrary, the zero point being fixed. We cannot, therefore, add a given number to each value of the variable and still maintain the properties of the original ratio scale. For example, the ratio of the two values 4 and 2 feet is $4/2 = 2$. If we add 5 feet to each of these two values, we have 9 and 7, and the ratio of $9/7$ is not equal to 2, the value we obtained previously. To add a given number to each of the values or to subtract a given number from each of the values changes the nature of the scale.

Since our unit of measurement on a ratio scale is arbitrary, we can multiply or divide each of our values by a specified number without changing the properties of the scale. Thus, multiplying our values of 4 feet and 2 feet by 12, to change our unit of measurement to inches, we have 48 and 24, and the ratio of $48/24$ equals 2, the same as before. In terms of inches, an object that is 48 inches long is still twice as long as the one that is 24 inches long.

Discrete and Continuous Variables

We have described briefly four types of scales used in classifying observations of variables: the nominal scale, the ordinal scale, the interval scale, and the ratio scale. All of these scales constitute forms of measurement to the scientist, but in ordinary everyday language what we usually mean by measurement are values of a variable that is *continuous*. When we deal with a nominal scale, we are concerned with a count or frequency, and these counts are always exact. We can have 9, 10, or 11 observations in a given class, but we cannot have 9.5 or 10.5 in a class. We say that frequencies are *discrete* because they can only fall at separated points on a scale, for example, at 0, 1, 2, 3, and so on.

Consider, however, measurements of length. If we are making observations of height, we ordinarily record our observations in terms of the nearest inch. If we measured the heights of a large number of different individuals, the values we would obtain would also fall at discrete points on a scale. Our unit of measurement is the inch, and it is generally considered sufficiently small in size to be appropriate for measurements of the heights of individuals. Obviously, however, we could have used a smaller unit of measurement, say 5/10 (or .5) of an inch, as our unit of measurement. Our measured values could still fall only at discrete points on our scale, at the values of 60.0, 60.5, 61.0, 61.5, and so on. If we measured in terms of a still smaller unit, say 1/100 (or .01) of an inch, we would still have values only at the discrete points 60.00, 60.01, 60.02, and so on. If we take still a smaller unit, 1/1,000 (or .001) of an inch, we would have potential values of 60.000, 60.001, 60.002, and so on. We note that no matter how small we make our unit of measurement, it can always, in theory at least, be made smaller. Between any two points of values on our scale, no matter how small the unit of measurement, we can always think of another value that would fall somewhere between these two values. Measurements on a scale such as this would correspond to measurements of a *continuous variable.*

Measurements of a continuous variable are always *approximations* of true values and are never exact. This is true of all continuous variables. Time may be measured in terms of years, months, weeks, days, hours, minutes, seconds, milliseconds, and so on, each succeeding unit being more precise than the one before, but even milliseconds are not exact values but only approximate. We have the interesting situation in which, although our variable is in theory continuous, the recorded values of our observations are in practice discrete.

Because of the approximate nature of measurements of continuous variables, we customarily, in analyzing data, regard a height reported in terms of the nearest inch, such as 61 inches, as representing an interval ranging from 60.5 up to 61.5, that is, half a unit of measurement below and half a unit above the value reported. If our unit of measurement is .1 of an inch, then an observation reported as 61.1 inches would be regarded as occupying an interval ranging from 61.05 up to 61.15, that is, half a unit below and half a unit above the reported value.

If heights are observed to the nearest .1 of an inch but reported only to the nearest inch, we say that we have rounded the number. In rounding to the nearest whole number, we drop the decimal fraction if it is less than .5 and report the whole number. If the decimal fraction is over .5, we raise the whole number by one. If the decimal fraction is exactly .5, it is customary to drop it if the whole number is an even number and report the even number. If the whole number is an odd number and the decimal fraction is .5, then the odd number is raised by one. The examples shown in Table 2.1 should make the accepted practice clear.

TABLE 2.1
Rounding Numbers

8.635	rounded to two decimal places becomes	8.64
8.625	rounded to two decimal places becomes	8.62
7.51	rounded to one decimal place becomes	7.5
7.55	rounded to one decimal place becomes	7.6
7.45	rounded to one decimal place becomes	7.4
7.49	rounded to one decimal place becomes	7.5
7.43	rounded to one decimal place becomes	7.4
5.9	rounded to the nearest whole number becomes	6
6.5	rounded to the nearest whole number becomes	6
7.5	rounded to the nearest whole number becomes	8
5.3	rounded to the nearest whole number becomes	5

Test Scores as Continuous Variables

Since many of the measurements made in psychology and education consist of test scores, we shall do well to consider something of the nature of the scale on which we assume our scores fall. To begin with, can we regard test scores as measurements of a continuous variable? Let us assume that we have an arithmetic test consisting of 50 items, and that the score on the test corresponds to the number of items answered correctly. Obviously, the scores can take only the discrete values of 0, 1, 2,

3, . . . , 50. Thus, in a sense, the test scores correspond to measurements of length or height, taken to the nearest inch. In dealing with test scores in later discussions, we shall assume that a reported score of say, 60, is to be regarded in the same manner as a reported height of 60 inches, that is, as occupying an interval ranging from 59.5 up to 60.5.

We know that, no matter whether we have an interval or a ratio scale for our test scores, the unit of measurement, which we have taken as one correct response, is arbitrary. Theoretically, we could pair our test items and take as our unit of measurement two correct responses, counting a single correct response to one member of a pair as 1/2 or .5 of a unit. If, at the same time, we increased our test length to 100 items, we would have possible scores of 0.0, 0.5, 1.0, 1.5, . . . , 50.0. Increasing the test to 500 items, taking as our unit of measurement 10 test items, and counting a correct response to a single item as .1 of a unit, we would have potential scores of 0.0, 0.1, 0.2, . . . , 50.0. Theoretically, then, we might regard test scores as measures of a continuous variable, provided we also assume that a correct response to any one item is equivalent to a correct response to any other item.

For scores on tests, the origin is obviously arbitrary, and, at best, the scores correspond to an interval scale, provided we can also assume that the distance or interval between a score of, say, 8 and 10, is equivalent to the distance between a score of 10 and 12. This assumption is the same as assuming that a correct response to a given item is equal to a correct response to any other item. Can we make this assumption about test scores? Can we assume that they constitute an interval scale?

Whether we choose to make this assumption or not apparently depends as much upon our personality as upon anything else. It is probably true that most psychometricians and others who deal with test scores would agree that we seldom, if ever, are right in assuming equivalence of responses to items in psychological tests. Yet practically all psychometricians proceed to make this assumption in analyzing test scores. If the assumption is incorrect, why is it made? In the first place, the psychometrician might argue that the test scores themselves are not influenced in any way by the assumptions we, as observers, make about them. They are only what they are. Furthermore, he might argue, anything we assume is, after all, only an assumption. An assumption is only an approximation of reality. If our assumptions correspond only in a rough way to reality, the correspondence may still be sufficiently good to lead to useful and pragmatic results. The development of psychological tests and the treatment of test scores as if they constituted an interval scale, he might argue, has led to very useful results in industry, education, government, and the armed forces. This alone is sufficient to justify the assumptions made.

We shall see that the psychometrician has a point. Although the methods we use in analyzing observations depend, in a way, upon the assumptions we make about the nature of our observations, the conclusions we draw from our analyses are, in many instances, unchanged by the failure of our observations to be in strict accordance with our assumptions.

Research Problems in Psychology and Education

Research problems consist essentially of defining issues clearly, making observations that are relevant to the issue, analyzing and describing the observations, and interpreting the results of the analyses as they bear upon the particular issue or question. Thus any question on which it is possible to make relevant observations can be made the basis of a research problem.

The following questions illustrate something of the scope of research activities in psychology and education. Will children, on the average, work harder when they are praised than when they are criticized? Is there any relationship between grades earned in college and scores on a college entrance examination? Does frustration result, on the average, in aggressive or regressive behavior or both? Will one method of teaching mathematics result in greater average achievement on the part of students than another method? Are boys more variable than girls in their performance on an achievement test? Do students, on the average, learn just as much from straight lectures as they do from discussion groups? In terms of average achievement, are small classes to be preferred to large classes? Are individuals who are honest in one situation likely to be honest in other situations? Are personality traits related to color of the hair? What is the greatest source of anxiety for college students? Do we tend to suppress experiences which are unpleasant? Is there any real difference between the results obtained by the counseling procedures used in "nondirective" therapy and "directive" therapy? To what extent can attitudes be changed as a result of viewing motion pictures? To what extent do "stereotypes" determine our responses to social issues? How can children's fears be eliminated most effectively? To what extent can children's intelligence-test scores be modified by changes in the environment? Do the attitudes we have toward various political concepts influence the meaning which these concepts have for us? Will students learn just as much from a lecture presented over TV as they will from the same lecture presented in the classroom? Will individuals who are said to have a high degree of anxiety respond differently to stress than individuals with a low degree of anxiety? Are psychological tests useful in predicting recovery from mental illness?

The posing of a question similar to those just listed is the first step in research. Questions, when properly phrased, become hypotheses which can then be subjected to empirical test. Once a question has been formulated, the next step is planning the experimental design. This consists of determining the relevance of various potential sets of observations that might be made to the variables in which we are interested, the manner in which the observations will be made, and the methods by which they will be analyzed. The third step is actually carrying out the research and the analysis. The final steps are interpreting the analyzed data and seeing that the results are then made available to other investigators.

Note, in the questions raised above, some of the problems involved. For example, in the first question, what do we mean by work? We must have in mind a response variable, but what observations shall we consider relevant to this variable. Do we mean work in a physical sense? By work "harder" do we mean "more persistently"? The meaning that we have attached to this variable will not be clear until we can *specify the observations* we are to make and the nature of the scale which we assume the observations comprise. With respect to "criticism" and "praise," we, perhaps, have in mind a condition of stimulation, but how shall we administer the "criticism" and "praise"? Again, this variable is not and will not be clearly defined for ourselves and for others until the condition of stimulation is specified.

The second question, merely by the form in which it is put, more clearly specifies the nature of the research problem. One variable will consist of college grades and the other scores on a college entrance examination. But do we mean all grades earned in college? Do we include grades in courses in physical education? Over what period of college attendance will the grades be based? Shall we demand at least one year of grades? Will grades in all courses be considered equivalent? Do we include both males and females? Graduate students? And what entrance examination is to be used in the research?

3. Statistical Analysis of Data

Arnold Lien

A. WHAT IS MEANT BY STATISTICAL METHODS?

Statistical methods may be defined as the presentation and analysis of numerical data collected through measurement.

... the ability to analyze data is one of the basic requirements in effective measurement and evaluation. A teacher may do his measurement with considerable insight and skill, but if he does not know how to organize and analyze this data, he will have a mass of meaningless impressions which will not aid him in determining where he has failed, and what to do next.

When data is collected, it is usually listed in random order in a column called the Raw Score Column. (See sample problem, Table 7) *Raw Scores* are nothing more than a series of scores presented in random order. The scores are counted, and the total *number of cases* (N) is recorded at the bottom of the column.

What is the highest score? In this grouping, it is 99. What is the lowest score? Here, it is 49. The range of scores is 50 points from 99 to 49. Then, what is the average score? Which score starts the upper quarter? Which score starts the lower quarter? Which scores are in the middle 50%? These questions cannot be answered accurately because the data is not organized properly.

Raw scores are of little value in understanding what the scores mean. However, one must have a starting point, and the raw score column is the starting point for the presentation and analysis of data. The next step in organizing the data for analysis is that of preparing a frequency distribution.

B. WHAT IS A SIMPLE FREQUENCY DISTRIBUTION AND HOW IS IT CONSTRUCTED?

A simple frequency distribution is graphic representation of a distribution of raw scores. Steps in the construction of a simple frequency distribution (Table 7) are these:

1. Make a Score Column (X). Place the scores in order of size from high to low listing each score value only once.
2. Make a Tally Column. Tabulate, by a vertical mark, the number of pupils receiving each score. Total tally column to be sure that this total coincides with the total number of raw scores.
3. Make a frequency column (f). Count the number of tallies for each score and enter this total as a number in f column. Total f column.

One can see that the raw scores now have been reorganized (presented) into a new framework for more efficient analysis. The teacher then can note at a glance the top score and the lowest score, can even approximate the average score, and can estimate the location of the top-quarter and of the lowest-quarter scores. However, the purpose of a simple frequency distribution chart is to *present* the scores—the first part of statistical analysis. The further columns in the simple frequency distribution charts are columns used for analysis of data.

C. WHAT IS THE FIRST STEP OF ANALYSIS?

Usually, the first step in analysis is to *rank* the scores. Later in this chapter, there is a section discussing correlation which describes the method used to rank scores.

TABLE 7
Simple Frequency Distribution

Raw Scores		Simple Frequency Distribution		
		X	Tally	f
77	62	99	/	1
84	57	93	/	1
67	87	87	/	1
77	67	84	////	4
73	73	77	ʬ/	5
93	62	73	///	3
84	77	67	///	3
62	67	62	///	3
77	84	57	/	1
49	N—24	52	/	1
73		49	/	1
99			N—24	N—24
84				
52				
77				

It may be well to note here that by ranking one determines the relative position of a score in a series of scores. This is accomplished by assigning the rank of 1 to the highest score (See Table 8) and then proceeding down the list of scores (remember the modification when there are duplicate scores). Ranking serves two purposes in analysis: first, it indicates the position of each score, and thus of each pupil, within the group; and second, it can be used as a means of grouping pupils into whatever numbers of sections desired.

D. WHAT ARE THE MEASURES OF CENTRAL TENDENCY AND HOW ARE THE BASIC ONES COMPUTED?

Measures of central tendency are points which represent all of the scores made by the group, and they give a concise description of the performance of the group as a whole. These measures are more commonly called *averages*. There are three basic averages: The mean, the median, and the mode.

1. What Is the Mean and How Is It Determined?
   a. Definition: The mean is the sum of the individual scores (ΣfX) divided by the number of cases (N). The mean is known as the *arithmetic average*.
   b. Formula:

$$M = \frac{\Sigma fX}{N}$$

Here, M means the mean, Σ stands for "sum of," ΣfX means the sum of the individual scores times the frequency of scores, and N equals the number of cases.

In the sample problem, the mean equals 74.

2. What Is the Median and How Is It Determined?
   a. Definition: The median is a point on either side of which there are an equal number of cases. This is known as the *counting average*.
   b. Formula:

$$\text{Mdn} = \frac{N + 1}{2} \quad \text{Result Count Up}$$

Here, *Mdn* stands for the Median, N + 1 for the number of cases.

The figure one obtains from the formula is not the median, but must be used to count upward into the distribution to find the median or middle point. In the illustrated problem, one counts upward from the bottom either in the frequency column or in the tally column. The twelfth frequency is on the score of 73 but there is still a .5 frequency remaining. It is important for the teacher at this point, to count downward from the top to be sure of the exact and correct point of the median. When counting downward from the top, the twelfth frequency is on 77 with .5 frequency remaining. This means that the median is midway between 73 and 77 which is 75.

Sometimes, the median is on an exact score; at other times, it will be the midpoint between two scores. When checking the first calculation by counting downward from the top, the median point can be determined accurately.

3. What Is the Mode and How Is It Determined?

    a. Definition: The *mode* is the score that occurs most frequently (the inspectional or observational average).

    b. Formula: The formula for the crude mode is its definition.

    In Table 8, one can observe the fact that the score of 77 has the greatest number of frequencies; therefore, the mode is 77.

TABLE 8
Measures of Central Tendency

X	f	Rank	fX
99	1	1	99
93	1	2	93
87	1	3	87
84	4	5.5	336
77	5	10	385
73	3	14	219
67	3	17	201
62	3	20	186
57	1	22	57
52	1	23	52
49	1	24	49
	N—24		1764

Mean	Median	Mode
$M = \dfrac{\Sigma fX}{N}$	$Mdn = \dfrac{N+1}{2}$	Score that occurs most frequently = 77
$= \dfrac{1764}{24}$	$= \dfrac{25}{2}$	
$= 73.5$	$= 12.5$ Count Up	
$= 74$	$= 75$	

c. Irregularities in determining the mode.

The mode is easily determined in a distribution in which one score has the greatest frequencies. It is not uncommon, however, for a distribution to have more than one score with the highest frequency. It is in this situation that the teacher must know how the mode is reported.

Following is the middle of the distribution with a new set of frequencies.

$$
\begin{array}{rl}
84 & - \;////\\
77 & - \;\cancel{////}\,/\\
73 & - \;///\\
67 & - \;\cancel{////}\,/\\
62 & - \;///
\end{array}
$$

Here, the highest number of frequencies is found at 77 and at 67. Since the two scores are not adjacent, the distribution is reported as *bimodal* (two modes), and it is reported as being 77 and 67.

Sometimes, there are more than two high points which have the same numbers of high frequencies, and they are not adjacent.

$$
\begin{array}{rl}
84 & - \;////\\
77 & - \;\cancel{////}\,/\\
73 & - \;///\\
67 & - \;\cancel{////}\,/\\
62 & - \;///\\
57 & - \;\cancel{////}\,/
\end{array}
$$

The three high points are 77, 67, and 57. This is called a multimodal distribution, and the three modes are reported. Any distribution of more than two modes is called multimodal.

The previous two paragraphs indicate how the modes are reported when the highest frequencies are not adjacent to each other. If the high frequencies *are all adjacent* to each other in either the bimodal or the multimodal distribution, it is normal to average these values and report the average as the modal point. If *all* high frequencies are not adjacent, however, the mode is reported as bimodal or multimodal as explained in the previous paragraphs.

Whenever there is more than one mode, it indicates that there is more than one point of concentration. It gives a clue to the teacher that there probably are various groups within the class. This can assist him in working with these groups for more individualized instruction.

E. WHEN ARE THE VARIOUS AVERAGES USED?

a. The mean is used when:

1. The measure of central tendency having the greatest reliability is desired. This means that the mean is the average which is most stable from sample to sample—it is the most consistent. The mean, therefore, is the average which is used most commonly.

2. Further statistical techniques are to be computed. Many times, the mean is a "prerequisite" to figuring a statistical result as in standard deviation or correlation coefficients.

3. Grades are to be determined using the mean as a reference point.

b. The median is used when:

1. There are extreme scores which would make the mean unreliable. For example, there are five teachers with salaries of $4600, $4700, $4800, $4900, and $7000. The mean would be $5200, but it would hardly be a representative average of the majority of the teachers. Here, the middle salary of $4800 (the median) would be a more representative average.

2. A quicker average is required for reporting purposes. Many times in reporting scores to pupils or parents, a teacher wants to report an average as a reference point. In most cases, the median can be obtained much more quickly than the mean and probably is accurate enough for a rough average. The author uses the median in reporting the average on check tests and other measurement which carry minimal weight.

3. Certain scores could influence the average, but all that is known about them is that they lie outside of the distribution. Sometimes, pupils do not complete a test in the allotted time and are marked DNC (did not complete), or they may receive such a high score that it "runs off the scale" at the upper end of the distribution. The median can easily be figured since each "score" counts only as one in finding the median point. The mean could not be figured since the exact value of each score must be known.

c. The mode is used when:
1. A quick, approximate measure of concentration is all that is needed.
2. The most frequently obtained score is desired. The mode is not a very reliable average as can be observed in its computation. There may be one mode, two modes, or many modes. Thus, it is not a decision as to whether to use the mode when a mean or median can be computed; rather, the decision is whether to use the mode as an additional index when using the mean or the median. Sometimes, it is of value in this situation. For example, the mean IQ of a class may be 110 and the mode is 100. This means that the arithmetic average (mean) indicates that the class, as a whole, has an average IQ at the upper end of the average range, but the greatest concentration of IQ's seems to be around the "normal" IQ of 100.

F. WHAT ARE MEASURES OF VARIABILITY AND HOW ARE THE BASIC ONES COMPUTED?

Measures of variability are indices which describe the spread or scatter of scores in a distribution. These measures are distances, not points. Sometimes, they are called ranges.

In comparing two sets of scores, one may find that the means are equal, but this does not mean that the distributions of the scores are identical. In Figure 5, the mean scores of both distributions are the same, 50. However, distribution A has scores ranging from 40 to 60, whereas distribution B has scores from 20 to 80. It is obvious, then, that the two groups are not identical and that they would require different approaches to teaching. To understand the differences within a distribution or between two distributions, it is necessary to know more than the average score.

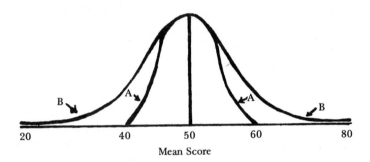

Figure 5. Mean Score of Two Distributions.

There are three basic measures of variability which a teacher may have an occasion to use or at least to understand in reading professional literature. These are the external range, the range by quartiles, and standard deviation.

1. The External Range
   a. Definition: The difference between the highest and the lowest score in the distribution.
   b. Formula: Range = H − L
      In a previous sample problem, the highest score was 99; the lowest was 49; therefore, the range is 50. (See Table 9)
      The range is useful because it indicates the variability of the group from one extreme to the other. A large range would mean a heterogeneous group on the measurement; a small range would mean a rather homogeneous group.

The external range is somewhat unreliable. It is influenced by the extreme scores only, and one extreme score can increase the external range by such an amount that it would not produce a reliable index of the variability of the majority of the group.

2. The Range by Quartiles

Because the external range gives the distance from one extreme to the other, sometimes one may obtain an erroneous picture of the variability within the distribution. To obtain further insight into the variability within the distribution, it might be desirable to determine the range by quartiles.

The range by quartiles is finding the range of the upper quarter, of the lowest quarter, and of the middle 50%. This must not be confused with quartile deviation, which is also an index of variability. The range by quartiles is useful in finding the variability of the groups within the distribution. It also can be used for dividing students into three sections for small-group instruction, for interpreting placement of pupils in the group, and for grading purposes. The last point will be explained further in Chapter 9, Marking and Reporting.

a. Range of the upper fourth

In order to find the range of the upper-fourth, it is necessary to locate the *point* which starts the upper-fourth. This point is known as the 75th percentile, or the point of Q_3.

Q_3 is determined by the same procedure as was used for the median or Q_2 except that, this time, one must count upward 75% of the way into the distribution. The formula is:

$Q_3 = 3/4N$ or $3N/4$. Result Count Up.

In the sample problem in Table 9, the N was 24. Therefore:

$Q_3 = 3/4$ of 24 or 18. Result Count Up.

By counting upward into the distribution 18 frequencies, the point of Q_3 is on 84. The point which begins the top quarter, then, is 84. The range of the top quarter in the distribution is 84-99; thus, a range of 15 points.

b. Range of the lowest fourth

Q_1 is the point below which lies the lower 25% of the cases, or the lowest fourth.
The formula is:

Q_1 = N/4. Result Count Up.

In the sample problem, the substitution would be:

Q_1 = 24/4 or 6. Result Count Up.

By counting upward six frequencies (and down 18 frequencies), one locates 64.5. The point of Q_1 is 64.5, but the lowest quarter range of actual scores is from 49-62, or a range of 13 points.

c. Range of the middle 50%

The range of the middle 50%, or the typical group, is easily determined then. It is between the starting points of the upper and lower quarters. In the sample problem in Table 9, the middle range would be between 67 and 77, or a range of 10 points.

The middle 50% of this sample group appears to be a very closely knit group with the difference being 10 points; the top quarter is only slightly greater in range than the lowest quarter (15 points as compared to 13).

Grade or class groups can be compared with one another through the use of the range by quartiles, and one can determine the quartile distributions within a single class or group. If one group had a range within the top quarter of 15 points and another group on the same measurement had a range of 30 points, the second group has a variability twice as great as the first group within the top quarter. The teaching procedures and the materials of instruction, therefore, would vary from one group to the other.

3. Standard Deviation

The standard deviation, or *SD*, is a measure of variability calculated around the mean. The *SD* is the most stable measure of variability and is customarily used in research problems and in studies involving correlation. The symbol for the *SD* is the Greek letter σ (sigma).[1]

TABLE 9
Measures of Variability

X	f	Rank	fX	d	fd	fd^2
99	1	1	99	25	25	625
93	1	2	93	19	19	361
87	1	3	87	13	13	169
84	4	5.5	336	10	40	400
77	5	10	385	3	15	45
73	3	14	219	−1	−3	3
67	3	17	201	−7	−21	147
62	3	20	186	−12	−36	432
57	1	22	57	−17	−17	289
52	1	23	52	−22	−22	484
49	1	24	49	−25	−25	625
	N = 24		1764			3580

Range	Top Fourth	Lower Fourth	Standard Deviation
$R = H - L$	$Q_3 = \dfrac{3N/4 \text{ Result}}{\text{Count Up}}$	$Q_1 = \dfrac{N/4 \text{ Result}}{\text{Count Up}}$	$SD = \sqrt{\dfrac{\Sigma fd^2}{N}}$
$= 99 - 49$	$= 72/4$	$= 24/4$	$= \sqrt{\dfrac{3580}{24}}$
$= 50$	$= 18$ Count Up	$= 6$ Count Up	$= \sqrt{149.17}$
	$= 84$	$= 64.5$	$= 12.21$
	$= 84 - 99$	$= 49 - 62$ (actual)	

---

[1] H. E. Garrett, *Elementary Statistics*, page 51. © Longmans, Green & Co., Inc., 1956.

Teachers will find *SD* used as a measure of variability when they read the manuals accompanying standardized tests and when they read research studies using statistical analysis. Teachers generally have not used *SD* in their own analysis of data primarily because it appeared to be a complex measure to compute and to interpret.

If one will realize, however, that *SD* is a unit of distance, it can be more readily understood. A foot is a unit of distance and, in measuring a room, the results are expressed in feet. Similarly, in a distribution of scores, the variability or distance can be stated in *SD* units.

$$\text{The formula is: } SD = \sqrt{\frac{\Sigma \, fd^2}{N}}$$

(where d stands for "deviation from the mean," f for frequency of scores, N for number of cases, and Σ for sum of.) In the sample problem in Table 9, the mean has been computed so that the deviation of each score from the mean is stated in the "d" column. Since some scores are duplicated, one multiplies the deviation by the frequency (fd) to obtain this column. Then fd^2 is obtained by multiplying the d column by the fd column. The resulting computation shows the *SD* value to be 12.21.

What does the *SD* value indicate about the nature of the distribution? Bartz states the value as follows:

Obviously, it tells *how much* the scores in a distribution deviate from the mean. If the value of the SD is small, there is little variability, and the majority of the scores are tightly clustered around the mean. If the SD is large, the scores are more widely scattered above and below the mean. The SD can be used for comparing two groups to see how they differ in variability.[2]

The *SD* statistic also can be used for placing grades in a distribution. More detailed information con-

---

[2] Albert E. Bartz, *Elementary Statistical Methods for Educational Measurement,* page 31. © Burgess Publishing Company, 1963.

cerning grade distribution will be presented in Chapter 9.

The importance of the *SD* cannot be overemphasized. Because the concept is basic to the construction and interpretation of tests, the teacher should familiarize himself thoroughly with the preceding discussion and calculations. Then, he should use these techniques to improve his analysis and thereby will improve his teaching procedures.

G. WHAT IS MEANT BY THE TECHNIQUE OF CORRELATION?

Definition:

Correlation is the degree of relationship which exists between two sets of scores.

Purpose:

The purpose is to reduce to a single number or index the relationship between two sets of scores. When this number or index is found, it is known as the *coefficient of correlation* and its symbol is p (rho) or r (depending on method used).

Uses of Correlation:

The basic uses of simple correlation are to check for the validity and for the reliability of an instrument. It may be used in guidance work as a means of predicting student progress or ability.

Kinds of Correlation:

There are basically two kinds of correlation.

Positive: When values or scores of one instrument go together *directly* with the values or scores of the other instrument, the correlation is positive. That is, the highs go with the highs, the middles with the middles, and the lows with the lows. The range of positive correlation is from +1.00 (perfect positive correlation) down through any fractional parts of positive 1 to zero.

Negative: When values or scores of one instrument go together *inversely* with the values or scores of the other instrument, the correlation is negative. That is, the highs of one go with the lows of the other. The range of negative correlation is from −1.00 (perfect negative correlation) down through any fractional parts of −1 to zero.

Range of Correlation Coefficients

−1.00	0	+1.00
Negative Range	Positive Range	

Formula for figuring correlation by the *Rank-Difference Method:*

The Rank-Difference Method of determining the coefficient of correlation is probably the simplest to use and can be done easily by teachers. All that is necessary is to add, subtract, multiply, and divide accurately. One additional skill, the ranking of scores, needs to be understood, and this will be explained in the problem to follow.

$$\rho = 1.00 - \left(\frac{6 \times \Sigma D^2}{N(N^2 - 1)} \right) \quad \text{(also known as } \rho \text{ or rho formula)}$$

The p stands for the coefficient of correlation; the 1.00 is a perfect correlation from which any value in the quantity may be taken to reduce the coefficient; the number 6 is a constant value; the combination of symbols ΣD^2 stands for the sum of the difference in ranks squared. In the denominator, N stands for the number of cases; the subquantity then stands for the number of cases squared—minus one.

Running a Correlation:

Suppose the teacher wanted to check the validity of a unit test (Column A) against a set of criterion scores which was an index of performance during the unit (Column B). In order to show the correlation in a simple way, one can use only ten cases; also the scores used will be in low figures. For the method to be used, see Table 10. Another formula for determining the coefficient of correlation, the Pearson *r*, or Product-Moment r, is found in Appendix C.

TABLE 10
Correlation Table

T-M Test A	Past Performance B	R_A	R_B	D	D^2
20	14	1	4	3	9.00
18	16	2	3	1	1.00
16	18	3	2	1	1.00
14	20	4	1	3	9.00
12	6	5	8	3	9.00
10	8	6	7	1	1.00
8	10	7	6	1	1.00
6	12	8	5	3	9.00
4	2	9	10	1	1.00
2	4	10	9	1	1.00
	N-10				42.00

$$\rho = 1.00 - \left(\frac{6 \times \Sigma D^2}{N(N^2-1)}\right)$$

$$\rho = 1.00 - \left(\frac{6 \times 42}{10(99)}\right)$$

$$\rho = 1.00 - \left(\frac{252}{990}\right)$$

$$\rho = 1.00 - .25$$

$$\rho = .75$$

Some explanation of the steps in this problem may be necessary. After the score columns (A and B), there are two columns, each headed R_A and R_B respectively. In each column, the rank of each score is determined. When scores are ranked, this is nothing more than giving its position in the series of scores (such as rank of 1 to the highest, rank of 2 to the next highest). Some difficulty in ranking can occur when there are duplicate scores in a column. This can be illustrated by an example.

In Column A, there are the following scores:

A	R_A	
20	1	Highest rank
18	2.5	The score of 18 is obtained by two pupils. They are entitled to the same rank, yet they take up two positions. Thus, position 2 plus position 3
18	2.5	is 5; divided by 2 (two pupils) = 2.5.
16	4	Three positions have been used to this point; thus, this is a single score receiving the next rank which is 4.
14	6	There are three 14's. They take up positions 5-6-7.
14	6	These added total 18; 18 divided by 3 (three pupils)
14	6	equals a rank of 6.
12	8	The next position is 8 for the single score.
10	9	Next position.
8	10	Last position.

N = 10

Accuracy of the ranking can be checked by noting whether the last rank given equals *N;* that is, number of cases. In this example, the last score received a rank of 10; 10 is also the number of cases. The only exception here is that, if the last score were duplicated, the rank given would be an average of the positions taken up. The rank given would not equal the absolute value of N but would be incorporated into the rank.

Another point which should be clarified in the problem is that of rounding of numbers. Notice that in the progression from the formula down to the answer, two decimal places are retained. There are many ways of rounding numbers; the main idea is that one must be consistent. These chapters will follow the principle that when the third digit is above 5, raise the previous digit; when the third digit is exactly 5 (that is, no remainder), look to the previous digit. If it is an even number, leave it as it is; if it is an odd number, raise it to the next number above. Generalizing in this latter instance, when rounding from an exact 5, always round to the even.

Interpreting the Coefficient of Correlation:

The correlation coefficient can vary from perfect positive, +1.00, to −1.00, a perfect negative correlation. Normally, these extreme values are uncommon in practice although correlations may approach these extremes. As the coefficient increases from 0.00 to +1.00, the relationship becomes greater; as it approaches −1.00, it also becomes greater, but in the negative direction. Coefficients of equal size but in opposite zones, positive or negative, are of equal strength but the direction of the correlation is different; that is, one is a direct relationship and the other is inverse or negative.

How high should a correlation be in order to be regarded as "significant"? Garrett answers the question in the following way.

It is difficult to answer this question categorically as the *level* of relationship indicated by r depends upon several factors: (1) the absolute size of the coefficient; (2) the purposes for which r is calculated and (3) how our r compares with r's generally found for the variables studied.[3]

A common guide which will assist the beginner in interpreting a coefficient of correlation is as follows:

± .70 to ± 1.00	High to very high
± .40 to ± .70	Average to fairly high
± .20 to ± .40	Present, but low
± .00 to ± .20	Negligible or low

For interpreting a coefficient of validity or of reliability, the reader is referred to Chapter 3 in which a discussion is presented on the factors to be considered in interpreting coefficients for these specific purposes.

---

[3]H. E. Garrett, *Elementary Statistics,* page 116. © Longmans, Green & Co., Inc., 1956.

A final principle to remember in interpreting correlation is that it does not show causation. If one would obtain a correlation of +.90 between the heights of boys and basketball performance, the relationship is high, but it does not follow that either is the cause of the other. It may be that other factors of health, coordination, and the like, causes both. Correlation may suggest the possibility of causal relationship, but it does no more than this. Proof of such causation would have to be determined by means other than correlation.

SUMMARY STATEMENTS

1. Statistical procedures include the presentation and analysis of numerical data collected through measurement (the analysis phase of measurement and evaluation).
2. Analysis of data is one of the basic skills which a teacher needs to develop because it is an indication where he has succeeded, where he has failed, and what he must do next.
3. A simple frequency distribution is the means by which one assembles a set of raw scores into a meaningful organization.
4. The first step of analysis is to determine the relative position of a score in a series of scores (ranking).
5. The second step of analysis is to determine a measure of central tendency. These measures are points which represent all of the scores made by the group and, as such, give a concise description of the performance of the group as a whole. The basic ones are the mean, median, and mode.
6. The third step of analysis is to determine a measure of variability. These measures are distances that describe the spread or scatter of scores in a distribution. The basic ones are the range, the variability by quartile, and standard deviation.
7. Correlation is the degree of relationship which exists between two sets of scores.
8. The basic uses of correlation are to check for the validity and for the reliability of an instrument.

Correlation may also be used in guidance work as a means of predicting pupil performance.

9. Generally, the higher the coefficient of correlation, the greater the relationship which exists between two sets of scores. Interpretation of the coefficient, however, depends on the absolute size of the r, the purpose for which the r is obtained, and how the r compared with r's generally obtained for the variables studied.

10. Correlation does not show causation. It may suggest the possibility of causal relationship, but it does no more than this.

4. The Concept of the Normal Curve

Susan McFarland

Let us begin with a hypothetical arithmetic test which we have given to a group of 85 students. In statistical terms, this test is a *variable,* which simply means it takes on different values for different individuals—it can vary. If we listed every possible score that could be made on the test and then made a tally mark opposite each possible score every time an individual made that score, we would have what is called a *frequency distribution.* Let us suppose that the lowest score which can be made on the arithmetic test is 15, while the highest score is 75. The possible *range* of scores on this test is 60 points, which is simply the difference between the lowest and highest scores.

Rather than listing all 85 of our scores, we can begin by dividing the range into equal-sized intervals (e.g., 10-19; 20-29; etc.) in order to reduce initially the size of our amount of information. We choose the size of our score intervals to lose as little information as possible while still making our mass of data more compact and more usable. We can then list the intervals we have chosen and make our tally.

Interval	Tally Marks	Frequency
10-19	〝〝〝	5
20-29	〝〝〝 〝〝〝	10
30-39	〝〝〝 〝〝〝 〝〝〝	15
40-49	〝〝〝 〝〝〝 〝〝〝 〝〝〝 〝〝〝	25
50-59	〝〝〝 〝〝〝 〝〝〝	15
60-69	〝〝〝 〝〝〝	10
70-79	〝〝〝	5

Frequency, then, merely refers to the number of cases falling in a particular score interval or at a particular score point.

If we wished to plot our data graphically, we could place our score intervals along the abscissa (or x-axis) and plot frequency along the ordinate (or y-axis).

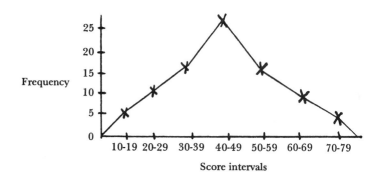

Figure 1. Frequency Polygon Representing Scores from Hypothetical Arithmetic Test.

Such a graph is known as a *frequency polygon* (Figure 1).

These same data could also be plotted as a *histogram,* which involves the use of bars constructed about the midpoint of each interval (Figure 2).

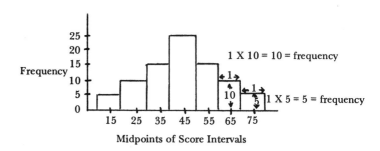

Figure 2. Histogram Representing Scores from Hypothetical Arithmetic Test.

If we arbitrarily assign the width of each bar in our histogram a value of 1, then the area of each bar in the histogram is representative of the frequency. Furthermore, it is possible to return the histogram to the form of a polygon by connecting the midpoints of each bar. As is shown in Figure 3, doing this does not change the area under the figure.

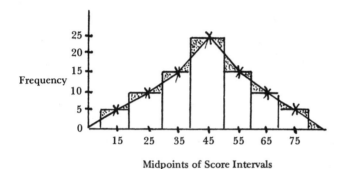

Midpoints of Score Intervals

Figure 3. Superimposed Histogram and Frequency Polygon Representing Scores from Hypothetical Arithmetic Test and Illustrating Principle of Equivalent Areas.

For every portion cut off from the histogram, an equivalent portion is added which was not previously included in the figure. Therefore, the area under the frequency polygon is equal to the area under the histogram, and proportionate areas under the respective figures are representative of proportionate frequencies.

The step from these notions to the concept of the normal distribution requires that we think in terms of giving our hypothetical test to an infinite number of people—instead of just giving it 85 times. Assuming that the irregularities in our frequency polygon stem from having a limited number of cases, we may say that as the number of cases approaches infinity, the polygon will become smoother and more regular and will approach the form of the normal curve, as shown in Figure 4.

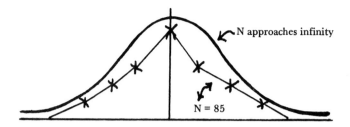

Figure 4. Hypothetical Removal of Irregularities as the Number of Cases Approaches Infinity.

With the normal distribution, as with the histogram and frequency polygon earlier, we can still utilize the notion of proportionate areas under the curve as indicators of proportionate frequencies.

Figure 5 shows the hypothetical normal distribution—the familiar bell-shaped curve which is the basis for much statistical theory and psychological and educational measurement. Two characteristics of this distribution are evident in Figure 5.

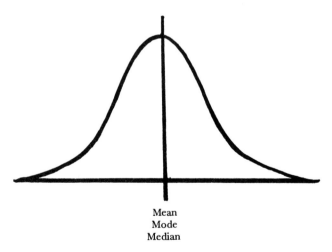

Mean
Mode
Median

Figure 5. Theoretical Normal Distribution Illustrating Symmetry and Identity of Mean, Mode and Median.

The normal distribution is symmetrical about its mid-point, and its mode, median and mean are identical. A perfectly precise pictorial presentation of the normal distribution would show a curve which never quite touches its baseline. Such a curve is said to be *asymptotic.* A somewhat oversimplified rationale for the asymptotic property of the normal distribution is that since it theoretically represents a population of infinite size, there must be allowance for any extreme values which might arise.

Finally, it should be stressed that the normal distribution does not exist in nature. It is an idealized mathematical distribution which has been found to be *approximated* frequently in nature. It has a wide range of applicability largely because it is useful.

5. Uses of the Standard Deviation

Abraham N. Franzblau

The standard deviation bears an interesting relationship to this curve of normal distribution and is, in fact, a mathematical function of that curve. Specifically, it is that point at which the curve changes from concave to convex, and vice versa. Mathematically, it is the point at which the slope of the curve changes its sign. It has been found that if we drop perpendiculars at these points of changing inflection on the curve, they will include between them approximately 68.26 per cent of the area under the curve. This is the same as saying that if we erect perpendiculars on the base line of the curve at a distance of plus and minus one standard deviation from the mean, the segment of the curve which they cut off will include 68.26 per cent of its area. Since the area of a curve consists merely of the piled-up frequencies of the distribution table from which the curve was drawn (as we have illustrated in Table 3), we can say that the points represented by −1 S.D. and +1 S.D., or ±σ mark the boundaries of the middle 68.26 per cent of any distribution of a trait found at random in nature.

To the beginner in statistics the figure 68.26 per cent will seem a strange one. The question may arise in his mind, Why was not some nice, round number selected instead to represent the area between ±1 S.D.? The question might be asked with as much justification about the constant π, which is known to equal 3.1416.

The answer is, in both cases, that the numbers represent facts of nature, like the number of teeth in the human mouth, or the weight of a cubic foot of water, or the speed of light. No one of these is an arbitrary figure selected by whim by some mathematician or scientist sitting in his armchair or ivory tower. Just as π represents the relationship between the circumference and the diameter of a circle, the latter fitting into the former 3.1416 times, so 68.26 per cent represents a corresponding relationship of the standard deviation to the curve of normal distribution. No matter how large the circumference of the circle, it will always be 3.1416 times its diameter—no more, no less. Similarly no matter how large the number of cases in a curve of normal distribution and no matter what the unit of measurement, 68.26 per cent of the cases will *always* be included between +1 S.D. and −1 S.D. as measured from the mean of the distribution.

It is very important to appreciate this fact and understand the constancy of this relationship under any and all circumstances. Needless to say, it holds true only for the curve of normal distribution. But since, as we have stated before, practically all traits measured at random in nature distribute in the shape of this curve, it can be readily seen how widely this relationship applies to the measurements we are likely to make and how helpful it is to understand this curve and its characteristics. Found so often, we accept it as a matter of routine unless we have definite evidence to the contrary.

If perpendiculars are erected at a distance of ±2σ from the mean, they include between them 95.46 per cent of all the cases; if at a distance of ±3σ, the perpendiculars include between them 99.78 per cent of all the cases. Since perpendiculars erected at ±4σ and ±5σ include in the third and fourth decimal places only a tiny fraction more of the total population, we usually say that the area of the curve is, for all practical purposes, contained between ±3σ. In fact, by the use of appropriate tables it is possible to discover what proportions of the curve of normal distribution are included between any two perpendiculars erected on the base line. In other words, once we know the properties of this curve (and there is a mathematical formula for it), we can determine the area of any slice of the curve just as easily as the slices cut at exactly 1σ, 2σ, or 3σ from the mean.

Another point which might be helpful is that since the standard deviation represents a *distance along the base line of the curve* as measured from the mean, we may represent not only whole σ units but fractions of them as well. Thus we deal with figures like $.5\sigma$, 1.78σ, 2.34σ, and the like. These have as precise a mathematical meaning as r in the formula πr^2 for the area of a circle.

Let us now examine the curve of normal distribution in the light of what we have learned. Curves, with perpendiculars erected at various σ distances along the base line, are shown in Figure 4.

We see from Charts A, B, and C in Figure 4 that perpendiculars erected at $+1\sigma$ and -1σ from the mean include between them 68.26 per cent of the area of the curve; at $+2\sigma$ and -2σ, 95.46 per cent of the area while at $+3\sigma$ and -3σ, almost all of the curve is included— actually, 99.78 per cent. Theoretically, to include the remaining .22 per cent of the area of the curve, it would be necessary to go out to infinity at either end. Hence, to all practical intents and purposes, we may say that the limits of $\pm 3\sigma$ include the entire area of the curve. We are ignoring only twenty-two ten-thousandths of it. At $\pm 4\sigma$, we are still ignoring one ten-thousandth.

Chart D in Figure 4 shows us how much of the area of the curve of normal distribution is included between each of the perpendiculars erected at any σ distance and the adjacent one. We see that the two middle segments each include 34.13 per cent of the cases, that the segments between $+1\sigma$ and $+2\sigma$ and between -1σ and -2σ each include 13.60 per cent, that those between $+2\sigma$ and $+3\sigma$ and between -2σ and -3σ contain 2.16 per cent each, while the end portions, from $+3\sigma$ to infinity (∞) and from -3σ to infinity, include .11 per cent each. If we wish to know the area of any segment of irregular size, we can find it by simple addition, as long as it is bounded by perpendiculars at any σ distance. Thus, for example, a segment bounded by $+1\sigma$

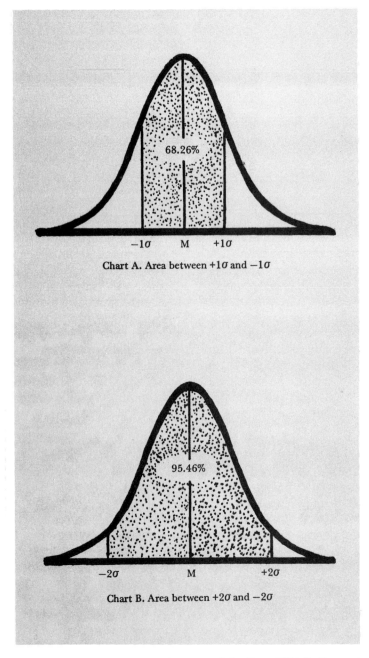

Chart A. Area between +1σ and −1σ

Chart B. Area between +2σ and −2σ

Figure 4. Areas of Various Segments of the Normal Distribution Curve.

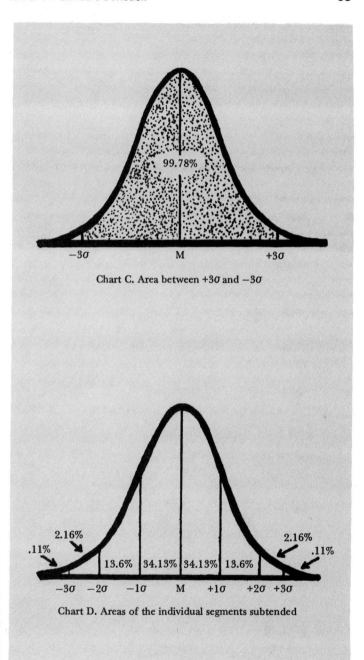

Chart C. Area between +3σ and −3σ

Chart D. Areas of the individual segments subtended

Figure 4 (cont.).

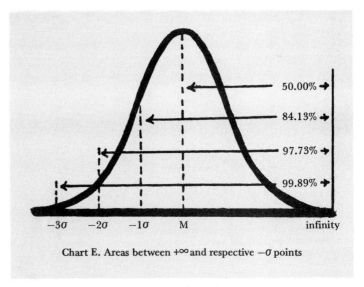

Chart E. Areas between $+\infty$ and respective $-\sigma$ points

Figure 4 (cont.).

and -2σ equals 34.13 per cent plus 34.13 per cent plus 13.60 per cent, or a total of 81.86 per cent. Similarly, a segment bounded by $+3\sigma$ and the mean equals 2.16 per cent plus 13.60 per cent plus 34.13 per cent, or a total of 49.89 per cent.

In Chart E we see the area of the segments which include one-half of the curve, stretching out to infinity, plus the -1σ, -2σ and -3σ segments, respectively. This is useful in determining what proportion of the population falls over or under a certain measure. In our example about the height of men, for instance, knowing that the mean height of the group is 5 feet 8.1 inches and that σ is 2 inches, we may easily calculate what proportion of men is above 5 feet 2 inches, in other words, 3σ below the mean. We see at once that in this group the percentage is 99.89.

Since these values are all mathematically rather than arbitrarily determined, tables can be constructed showing the area of any portions of the curve, even when the boundaries are erected at points representing fractions of a σ. Such tables are readily available in all advanced books on statistics as well as in separate publications containing only tables—Barlow's or Sheppard's Tables, for instance.

The importance of these calculations is great. If we find, for example, that the mean height of the men in a certain group is 5 feet 8 inches, with a standard deviation of 2 inches, we can tell without any difficulty or computation that only about 16 per cent of the men are shorter than 5 feet 6 inches; that is, only 15.87 per cent of the curve falls below a perpendicular erected at -1σ from the mean, 5 feet 6 inches being 2 inches, or 1σ, below the mean. Similarly, we know at a glance that only about 16 per cent of the men are apt to be taller than 5 feet 10 inches. (We round off the decimals wherever possible.)

Again, we know automatically that only 2.3 per cent of the men are apt to be taller than 6 feet (namely, 4 inches, or 2σ above the mean height). We also know that practically all of the men will range between 5 feet 2 inches and 6 feet 2 inches (that is, 99.8 per cent of the area is included between $\pm3\sigma$, or 6 inches, measured either side of the mean).

The same reasoning enables us to tell the approximate placement of any man in this group. Let us assume that a man is 6 feet tall; what is his approximate position in the group in order of height? Six feet is 4 inches, or 2σ, above the mean height; therefore only 2.3 per cent of men are apt to be taller than this man. Or suppose a man is 5 feet 6 inches tall; what is his position in the group? Five feet 6 inches is 2 inches, or 1σ, below the mean; hence 84 per cent of men will be taller than he is.

Another important use of the standard deviation is to compare measures of several different traits on a common basis. Suppose we have measured a man on four traits and find his measurements to be shown in Table 10.

Mr. A's measurements alone tell us very little. However, if we examine them in the light of the means and standard deviations of all men, they take on new significance. Thus his height is 4 inches, or 2σ, below the average; his chest expansion is 2 inches, or 2σ, above the average; and his intelligence 20 points, or 1σ, below the average. Whereas the figures alone tell us nothing as to his relative standing among other men, the standard deviations and means enable us to secure an idea of how his various traits compare. We see that he is very short, heavier than we would expect for his height, big-chested, and not overly bright.

TABLE 10
Use of Standard Deviation for Comparison of Various Traits

	Measurements of Mr. A		Measurements of All Men	
Trait	Measurement	Mean		Standard deviation
Height	5 feet 4 inches	5 feet 8 inches		2 inches
Weight	130 pounds	150 pounds		20 pounds
Chest expansion	6 inches	4 inches		1 inch
Intelligence quotient	80	100		20

The following illustration will show another important application which can be made of the standard deviation. Let us suppose that a man comes to us for advice as to whether he has sufficient intelligence to succeed in either medicine, dentistry, or pharmacy. Since large numbers of men in these professions were given an intelligence test during the war, we now have a fairly good idea of the distribution of the intelligence test scores of such men. The facts in this particular case, let us imagine, are as shown in Table 11.

TABLE 11
Use of Standard Deviation for Comparison with Groups

Profession	Average intelligence test score	Standard deviation
Medicine	165	15
Dentistry	155	20
Pharmacy	135	25

Mr. X's intelligence test score is 135.

What advice shall we give him? The standard deviations and means come to our help. Mr. X's score of 135 is 30 points below the mean of physicians, which is a deviation of -2σ. In other words, 98 per cent of physicians score higher than he. Obviously his chances in this field, when based on intelligence test scores, are very slim. Among dentists a score of 135 is 20 points, or 1σ, below the mean. This means that 84 per cent of dentists score higher than he. Yet, by the same token, 16 per cent of them do not score as high, which would indicate a small chance of success if he were content always to be in the tail end of his profession. In pharmacy, however, a score of 135 falls exactly at the mean. In other words, he scores higher than 50 per cent of pharmacists, although another 50 per cent may score higher than he. This points to at least an even chance for him in this profession and, insofar as we might be guided by intelligence test scores, would probably influence us to advise him to study pharmacy in preference to the two other professions. Needless to say, this illustration is hypothetical; in reality, many other factors would enter the picture.

6. How to Talk Back to a Statistic

Darrell Huff
Irving Geis

So far, I have been addressing you rather as if you were a pirate with a yen for instruction in the finer points of cutlass work. In this concluding chapter I'll drop that literary device. I'll face up to the serious purpose that I like to think lurks just beneath the surface of this book: explaining how to look a phony statistic in the eye and face it down; and no less important, how to recognize sound and usable data in that wilderness of fraud to which the previous chapters have been largely devoted.

Not all the statistical information that you may come upon can be tested with the sureness of chemical analysis or of what goes on in an assayer's laboratory. But you can prod the stuff with five simple questions, and by finding the answers avoid learning a remarkable lot that isn't so.

Who Says So?

About the first thing to look for is bias—the laboratory with something to prove for the sake of a theory, a reputation, or a fee; the newspaper whose aim is a good story; labor or management with a wage level at stake.

Look for conscious bias. The method may be direct misstatement or it may be ambiguous statement that serves as well and cannot be convicted. It may be

Reprinted from *How to Lie With Statistics* by Darrell Huff. Pictures by Irving Geis. By permission of W. W. Norton and Co., Inc. Copyright ©1954 by Darrell Huff and Irving Geis.

selection of favorable data and suppression of unfavorable. Units of measurement may be shifted, as with the practice of using one year for one comparison and sliding over to a more favorable year for another. An improper measure may be used: a mean where a median would be more informative (perhaps all too informative), with the trickery covered by the unqualified word "average."

Look sharply for unconscious bias. It is often more dangerous. In the charts and predictions of many statisticians and economists in 1928 it operated to produce remarkable things. The cracks in the economic structure were joyously overlooked, and all sorts of evidence was adduced and statistically supported to show that we had no more than entered the stream of prosperity.

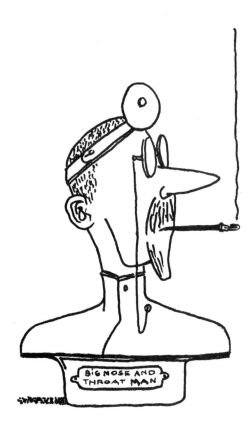

It may take at least a second look to find out who-says-so. The who may be hidden by what Stephen Potter, the *Lifemanship* man, would probably call the "O.K. name." Anything smacking of the medical profession is an O.K. name. Scientific laboratories have O.K. names. So do colleges, especially universities, more especially ones eminent in technical work. The writer who proved a few chapters back that higher education jeopardizes a girl's chance to marry made good use of the O.K. name of Cornell. Please note that while the data came from Cornell, the conclusions were entirely the writer's own. But the O.K. name helps you carry away a misimpression of "Cornell University says . . ."

When an O.K. name is cited, make sure that the authority stands behind the information, not merely somewhere alongside it.

You may have read a proud announcement by the Chicago *Journal of Commerce*. That publication had made a survey. Of 169 corporations that replied to a poll on price gouging and hoarding, two-thirds declared that they were absorbing price increases produced by the Korean war. "The survey shows," said the *Journal* (look sharp whenever you meet those words!), "that corporations have done exactly the opposite of what the enemies of the American business system have charged." This is an obvious place to ask, "Who says so?" since the *Journal of Commerce* might be regarded as an interested party. It is also a splendid place to ask our second test question:

How Does He Know?

It turns out that the *Journal* had begun by sending its questionnaires to 1,200 large companies. Only fourteen per cent had replied. Eighty-six per cent had not cared to say anything in public on whether they were hoarding or price gouging.

The *Journal* had put a remarkably good face on things, but the fact remains that there was little to brag about. It came down to this: Of 1,200 companies polled, nine per cent said they had not raised prices, five per cent said they had, and eighty-six per cent wouldn't say. Those that had replied constituted a sample in which bias might be suspected.

Watch out for evidence of a biased sample, one that has been selected improperly or—as with this one—has selected itself. Ask the question we dealt with in an early chapter: Is the sample large enough to permit any reliable conclusion?

Similarly with a reported correlation: Is it big enough to mean anything? Are there enough cases to add up to any significance? You cannot, as a casual reader, apply tests of significance or come to exact conclusions as to the adequacy of a sample. On a good many of the things you see reported, however, you will be able to tell at a glance—a good long glance, perhaps—that there just weren't enough cases to convince any reasoning person of anything.

What's Missing?

You won't always be told how many cases. The absence of such a figure, particularly when the source is an interested one, is enough to throw suspicion on the whole thing. Similarly a correlation given without a measure of reliability (probable error, standard error) is not to be taken very seriously.

Watch out for an average, variety unspecified, in any matter where mean and median might be expected to differ substantially.

Many figures lose meaning because a comparison is missing. An article in *Look* magazine says, in connection with Mongolism, that "one study shows that in 2,800 cases, over half of the mothers were 35 or over." Getting any meaning from this depends upon your knowing something about the ages at which women in general produce babies. Few of us know things like that.

Here is an extract from the *New Yorker* magazine's "Letter from London" of January 31, 1953.

> The Ministry of Health's recently published figures showing that in the week of the great fog the death rate for Greater London jumped by twenty-eight hundred were a shock to the public, which is used to regarding Britain's unpleasant climatic effects as nuisances rather than as killers. . . . The extraordinary lethal properties of this winter's prize visitation . . .

But how lethal *was* the visitation? Was it exceptional for the death rate to be that much higher than usual in a week? All such things do vary. And what about ensuing weeks? Did the death rate drop below average, indicating that if the fog killed people they were largely those who would have died shortly anyway? The figure sounds impressive, but the absence of other figures takes away most of its meaning.

Sometimes it is percentages that are given and raw figures that are missing, and this can be deceptive too. Long ago, when Johns Hopkins University had just begun to admit women students, someone not particularly enamored of coeducation reported a real shocker: Thirty-three and one-third per cent of the women at Hopkins had married faculty members! The raw figures gave a clearer picture. There were three women enrolled at the time, and one of them had married a faculty man.

A couple of years ago the Boston Chamber of Commerce chose its American Women of Achievement. Of the sixteen among them who were also in *Who's Who,* it was announced that they had "sixty academic degrees and eighteen children." That sounds like an informative picture of the group until you discover that among the women were Dean Virginia Gildersleeve and Mrs. Lillian M. Gilbreth. Those two had a full third of the degrees between them. And Mrs. Gilbreth, of course, supplied two-thirds of the children.

A corporation was able to announce that it's stock was held by 3,003 persons, who had an average of 660 shares each. This was true. It was also true that of the two million shares of stock in the corporation three men held three-quarters and three thousand persons held the other one-fourth among them.

If you are handed an index, you may ask what's missing there. It may be the base, a base chosen to give a distorted picture. A national labor organization once showed that indexes of profits and production had risen much more rapidly after the depression than an index of wages had. As an argument for wage increases this

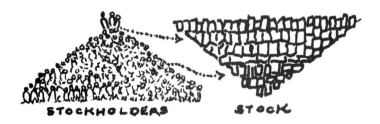

STOCKHOLDERS   STOCK

demonstration lost its potency when someone dug out the missing figures. It could be seen then that profits had been almost bound to rise more rapidly in percentage than wages simply because profits had reached a lower point, giving a smaller base.

Sometimes what is missing is the factor that caused a change to occur. This omission leaves the implication that some other, more desired, factor is responsible. Figures published one year attempted to show that business was on the upgrade by pointing out that April retail sales were greater than in the year before. What was missing was the fact that Easter had come in March in the earlier year and in April in the later year.

A report of a great increase in deaths from cancer in the last quarter-century is misleading unless you know how much of it is a product of such extraneous factors as these: Cancer is often listed now where "causes unknown" was formerly used; autopsies are more frequent, giving surer diagnoses reporting and compiling of medical statistics are more complete; and people more frequently reach the most susceptible ages now. And if you are looking at total deaths rather than the death rate, don't neglect the fact that there are more people now than there used to be.

Did Somebody Change the Subject?

When assaying a statistic, watch out for a switch somewhere between the raw figure and the conclusion. One thing is all too often reported as another.

As just indicated, more reported cases of a disease are not always the same thing as more cases of the disease. A straw-vote victory for a candidate is not always negotiable at the polls. An expressed preference by a "cross section" of a magazine's readers for articles on world affairs is no final proof that they would read the articles if they were published.

Encephalitis cases reported in the central valley of California in 1952 were triple the figure for the worst previous year. Many alarmed residents shipped their children away. But when the reckoning was in, there had been no great increase in deaths from sleeping sickness. What had happened was that state and federal health people had come in in great numbers to tackle a long-time problem; as a result of their efforts a great many low-grade cases were recorded that in other years would have been overlooked, possibly not even recognized.

It is all reminiscent of the way that Lincoln Steffens and Jacob A. Riis, as New York newspapermen, once created a crime wave. Crime cases in the papers reached such proportions, both in numbers and in space and big type given to them, that the public demanded action. Theodore Roosevelt, as president of the reform Police Board, was seriously embarrassed. He put an end to the crime wave simply by asking Steffens and Riis to lay off. It had all come about simply because the reporters, led by those two, had got into competition as to who could dig up the most burglaries and whatnot. The official police record showed no increase at all.

"The British male over 5 years of age soaks himself in a hot tub on an average of 1.7 times a week in the winter and 2.1 times in the summer," says a newspaper story. "British women average 1.5 baths a week in the winter and 2.0 in the summer." The source is a Ministry of Works hot-water survey of "6,000 representative British homes." The sample was representative, it says,

and seems quite adequate in size to justify the conclusion in the San Francisco *Chronicle's* amusing headline: BRITISH HE'S BATHE MORE THAN SHE'S.

The figures would be more informative if there were some indication of whether they are means or medians. However, the major weakness is that the subject has been changed. What the Ministry really found out is how often these people said they bathed, not how often they did so. When a subject is as intimate as this one is, with the British bath-taking tradition involved, saying and doing may not be the same thing at all. British he's may or may not bathe oftener than she's; all that can safely be concluded is that they say they do.

Here are some more varieties of change-of-subject to watch out for.

A back-to-the-farm movement was discerned when a census showed half a million more farms in 1935 than five years earlier. But the two counts were not talking about the same thing. The definition of farm used by the Bureau of the Census had been changed; it took in at least 300,000 farms that would not have been so listed under the 1930 definition.

Strange things crop out when figures are based on what people say—even about things that seem to be objective facts. Census reports have shown more people at thirty-five years of age, for instance, than at either thirty-four or thirty-six. The false picture comes from one family member's reporting the ages of the others and, not being sure of the exact ages, tending to round them off to a familiar multiple of five. One way to get around this: ask birth dates instead.

The "population" of a large area in China was 28 million. Five years later it was 105 million. Very little of that increase was real; the great difference could be explained only by taking into account the purposes of the two enumerations and the way people would be inclined to feel about being counted in each instance. The first census was for tax and military purposes, the second for famine relief.

Something of the same sort has happened in the United States. The 1950 census found more people in the sixty-five-to-seventy age group than there were in the fifty-five-to-sixty group ten years before. The difference could not be accounted for by immigration. Most of it could be a product of large-scale falsifying of ages by people eager to collect social security. Also possible is that some of the earlier ages were understated out of vanity.

Another kind of change-of-subject is represented by Senator William Langer's cry that "we could take a prisoner from Alcatraz and board him at the Waldorf-Astoria cheaper. . . ." The North Dakotan was referring to earlier statements that it cost eight dollars a day to maintain a prisoner at Alcatraz, "the cost of a room at a good San Francisco hotel." The subject has been changed from total maintenance cost (Alcatraz) to hotel-room rent alone.

The *post hoc* variety of pretentious nonsense is another way of changing the subject without seeming to. The change of something *with* something else is presented as *because of*. The magazine *Electrical World* once offered a composite chart in an editorial on "What Electricity Means to America." You could see from it that as "electrical horsepower in factories" climbed, so did "average wages per hour." At the same time "average hours per week" dropped. All these things are long-time trends, of course, and there is no evidence at all that any one of them has produced any other.

And then there are the firsters. Almost anybody can claim to be first in *something* if he is not too particular what it is. At the end of 1952 two New York newspapers were each insisting on first rank in grocery advertising. Both were right too, in a way. The *World-Telegram* went on to explain that it was first in full-run advertising, the kind that appears in all copies, which is the only kind it runs. The *Journal-American* insisted that total linage was what counted and that it was first in that. This is the kind of reaching for a superlative that leads the weather reporter on the radio to label a quite normal day "the hottest June second since 1949."

Change-of-subject makes it difficult to compare cost when you contemplate borrowing money either directly or in the form of installment buying. Six per cent sounds like six per cent—but it may not be at all.

If you borrow $100 from a bank at six per cent interest and pay it back in equal monthly installments for a year, the price you pay for the use of the money is about $3. But another six per cent loan, on the basis sometimes called $6 on the $100, will cost you twice as much. That's the way most automobile loans are figured. It is very tricky.

The point is that you don't have the $100 for a year. By the end of six months you have paid back half of it. If you are charged at $6 on the $100, or six per cent of the amount, you really pay interest at nearly twelve per cent.

Even worse was what happened to some careless purchasers of freezer-food plans in 1952 and 1953. They were quoted a figure of anywhere from six to twelve per cent. It sounded like interest, but it was not. It was an on-the-dollar figure and, worst of all, the time was often six months rather than a year. Now $12 on the $100 for money to be paid back regularly over half a year works out to something like forty-eight per cent real interest. It is no wonder that so many customers defaulted and so many food plans blew up.

Sometimes the semantic approach will be used to change the subject. Here is an item from *Business Week* magazine.

> Accountants have decided that "surplus" is a nasty word. They propose eliminating it from corporate balance sheets. The Committee on Accounting Procedure of the American Institute of accountants says: . . . Use such descriptive terms as "retained earnings" or "appreciation of fixed assets."

This one is from a newspaper story reporting Standard Oil's record-breaking revenue and net profit of a million dollars a day.

> Possibly the directors may be thinking some time of splitting the stock for there may be an advantage . . . if the profits per share do not look so large. . . .

Does It Make Sense?

"Does it make sense?" will often cut a statistic down to size when the whole rigamarole is based on an unproved assumption. You may be familiar with the Rudolf Flesch readability formula. It purports to measure how easy a piece of prose is to read, by such simple and objective items as length of words and sentences. Like all devices for reducing the imponderable to a number and substituting arithmetic for judgment, it is an appealing idea. At least it has appealed to people who employ writers, such as newspaper publishers, even if not to many writers themselves. The assumption in the formula is that such things as word length determine readability. This, to be ornery about it, remains to be proved.

A man named Robert A. Dufour put the Flesch formula on trial on some literature that he found handy. It showed "The Legend of Sleepy Hollow" to be half again as hard to read as Plato's *Republic*. The Sinclair Lewis novel *Cass Timberlane* was rated more difficult than an essay by Jacques Maritain, "The Spiritual Value of Art." A likely story.

Many a statistic is false on its face. It gets by only because the magic of numbers brings about a suspension of common sense. Leonard Engel, in a *Harper's* article, has listed a few of the medical variety.

An example is the calculation of a well-known urologist that there are eight million cases of cancer of the prostate gland in the United States— which would be enough to provide 1.1 carcinomatous prostate glands for every male in the susceptible age group! Another is a prominent neurologist's estimate that one American in twelve suffers from migraine; since migraine is responsible for a third of chronic headache cases, this would mean that a quarter of us must suffer from disabling headaches. Still another is the figure of 250,000 often given for the number of multiple sclerosis cases; death data indicate that there can be, happily, no more than thirty to forty thousand cases of this paralytic disease in the country.

Hearings on amendments to the Social Security Act have been haunted by various forms of a statement that makes sense only when not looked at closely. It is an argument that goes like this: Since life expectancy is only about sixty-three years, it is a sham and a fraud to set up a social-security plan with a retirement age of sixty-five, because virtually everybody dies before that.

You can rebut that one by looking around at people you know. The basic fallacy, however, is that the figure refers to expectancy at birth, and so about half the babies born can expect to live longer than that. The figure, incidentally, is from the latest official complete life table and is correct for the 1939-1941 period. An up-to-date estimate corrects it to sixty-five-plus. Maybe that will produce a new and equally silly argument to the effect that practically everybody now lives to be sixty-five.

Postwar planning at a big electrical-appliance company was going great guns a few years ago on the basis of a declining birth rate, something that had been taken for granted for a long time. Plans called for emphasis on small-capacity appliances, apartment-size refrigerators. Then one of the planners had an attack of common sense: He came out of his graphs and charts long enough to notice that he and his co-workers and his friends and his neighbors and his former classmates with few exceptions either had three or four children or planned to. This led to some open-minded investigating and charting—and the company shortly turned its emphasis most profitably to big-family models.

The impressively precise figure is something else that contradicts common sense. A study reported in New

York City newspapers announced that a working woman living with her family needed a weekly pay check of $40.13 for adequate support. Anyone who has not suspended all logical processes while reading his paper will realize that the cost of keeping body and soul together cannot be calculated to the last cent. But there is a dreadful temptation; "$40.13" sounds so much more knowing than "about $40."

You are entitled to look with the same suspicion on the report, some years ago, by the American Petroleum Industries Committee that the average yearly tax bill for automobiles is $51.13.

Extrapolations are useful, particularly in that form of soothsaying called forecasting trends. But in looking at the figures or the charts made from them, it is necessary to remember one thing constantly: The trend-to-now may be a fact, but the future trend represents no more than an educated guess. Implicit in it is "everything else being equal" and "present trends continuing." And somehow everything else refuses to remain equal, else life would be dull indeed.

For a sample of the nonsense inherent in uncontrolled extrapolation, consider the trend of television. The number of sets in American homes increased around 10,000% from 1947 to 1952. Project this for the next five years and you find that there'll soon be a couple billion of the things, Heaven forbid, or forty sets per family. If you want to be even sillier, begin with a base year that is earlier in the television scheme of things than 1947 and you can just as well "prove" that each family will soon have not forty but forty thousand sets.

A Government research man, Morris Hansen, called Gallup's 1948 election forecasting "the most publicized statistical error in human history." It was a paragon of accuracy, however, compared with some of our most widely used estimates of future population, which have earned a nationwide horselaugh. As late as 1938 a presidential commission loaded with experts doubted that the U.S. population would ever reach 140 million; it was 12 million more than that just twelve years later. There are textbooks published so recently that they are still in college use that predict a peak population of not more than 150 million and figure it will take until about 1980 to reach it. These fearful underestimates came from assuming that a trend would continue without change. A similar assumption a century ago did as badly in the opposite direction because it assumed continuation of the population-increase rate of 1790 to 1860. In his second message to Congress, Abraham Lincoln predicted the U.S. population would reach 251,689,914 in 1930.

Not long after that, in 1874, Mark Twain summed up the nonsense side of extrapolation in *Life on the Mississippi:*

In the space of one hundred and seventy-six years the Lower Mississippi has shortened itself two hundred and forty-two miles. That is an average of a trifle over one mile and a third per year. Therefore, any calm person, who is not blind or idiotic, can see that in the Old Oolitic Silurian Period, just a million years ago next November, the Lower Mississippi River was upward of one million three hundred thousand miles long, and stuck out over the Gulf of Mexico like a fishing-rod. And by the same token any person can see that seven hundred and forty-two years from now the Lower Mississippi will be only a mile and three-quarters long, and Cairo and New Orleans will have joined their streets together, and be plodding comfortably along under a single mayor and a mutual board of aldermen. There is something fascinating about science. One gets such wholesale returns of conjecture out of such a trifling investment of fact.

II. Classroom Testing

7. Measurement and the Teacher

Robert L. Ebel

The principles of measurement of educational achievement presented in this article are based on the experience and research of a great many people who have been working to improve classroom testing. The particular principles discussed here were selected on the basis of their relevance to the questions and problems that arise most often when tests of educational achievement are being considered, prepared and used. While some of the principles may seem open to question, we believe a case can be made in support of each one.

1. *The measurement of educational achievement is essential to effective education.* Learning is a natural, inevitable result of human living. Some learning would occur even if no special provision were made for it in schools, or no special effort were taken to facilitate it. Yet efficient learning of complex achievements, such as reading, understanding of science, or literary appreciation, requires special motivation, guidance and assistance. Efforts must be directed toward the attainment of specific goals. Students, teachers and others involved in the process of education must know to what degree the goals have been achieved. The measurement of educational achievement can contribute to these activities.

Robert L. Ebel. "Measurement and the Teacher." *Educational Leadership,* 20: 20–24. October, 1962. Reprinted with permission of the Association for Supervision and Curriculum Development and Robert L. Ebel. Copyright ©1962 by the Association for Supervision and Curriculum Development.

It is occasionally suggested that schools could get along without tests, or indeed that they might even do a better job if testing were prohibited. It is seldom if ever suggested, though, that education can be carried on effectively by teachers and students who have no particular goals in view, or who do not care what or how much is being learned. If tests are outlawed, some other means of assessing educational achievement would have to be used in their place.

2. An educational test is no more or less than a device for facilitating, extending and refining a teacher's observations of student achievement. In spite of the Biblical injunction, most of us find ourselves quite often passing judgments on our fellow men. Is candidate *A* more deserving of our vote than candidate *B*? Is *C* a better physician than *D*? Is employee *E* entitled to a raise or a promotion on his merits? Should student *F* be given a failing mark? Should student *L* be selected in preference to student *M* for the leading role in the class play?

Those charged with making such judgments often feel they must do so on the basis of quite inadequate evidence. The characteristics on which the decision should be based may not have been clearly defined. The performances of the various candidates may not have been observed extensively, or under comparable conditions. Instead of recorded data, the judge may have to trust his fallible memory, supplemented with hearsay evidence.

Somewhat similar problems are faced by teachers, as they attempt to assess the achievements of their students. In an effort to solve these problems, tests have been developed. Oral examinations and objective examinations are means for making it easier for the teacher to observe a more extensive sample of student behavior under more carefully controlled conditions.

The price that must be paid for a test's advantages of efficiency and control in the observation of student achievements is some loss in the naturalness of the behavior involved. In tests which attempt to measure the student's typical behavior, especially those aspects of behavior which depend heavily on his interests, attitudes, values or emotional reactions, the artificiality of the test situation may seriously distort the measurements obtained. But this problem is much less serious in tests intended to measure how much the student knows, and what he can do with his knowledge. What is gained in efficiency and precision of measurement usually far outweighs what may be lost due to artificiality of the situation in which the student's behavior is observed.

3. *Every important outcome of education can be measured.* In order for an outcome of education to be important, it must make a difference. The behavior of a person who has more of a particular outcome must be observably different from that of a person who has less. Perhaps one can imagine some result of education which is so deeply personal that it does not ever affect in any way what he says or does, or how he spends his time. But it is difficult to find any grounds for arguing that such a well concealed achievement is important.

If the achievement does make a difference in what a person can do or does do, then it is measurable. For the most elementary type of measurement requires nothing more than the possibility of making a verifiable observation that person or object X has more of some defined characteristic than person or object Y.

To say that any important educational outcome is measurable is not to say that satisfactory methods of measurement now exist. Certainly it is not to say that every important educational outcome can be measured by means of a paper and pencil test. But it is to reject the claim that some important educational outcomes are too complex or too intangible to be measured. Importance and measurability are logically inseparable.

4. *The most important educational achievement is command of useful knowledge.* If the importance of an educational outcome may be judged on the basis of what teachers and students spend most of their time doing, it is obvious that acquisition of a command of useful knowledge is a highly important outcome. Or if one asks how the other objectives are to be attained—objectives of self-realization, of human relationship, of economic efficiency, of civic responsibility—it is obvious again that command of useful knowledge is the principle means.

How effectively a person can think about a problem depends largely on how effectively he can command the knowledge that is relevant to the problem. Command of knowledge does not guarantee success, or happiness, or righteousness, but it is difficult to think of anything else a school can attempt to develop which is half as likely to lead to these objectives.

If we give students command of knowledge, if we develop their ability to think, we make them intellectually free and independent. This does not assure us that they will work hard to maintain the status quo, that they will adopt all of our beliefs and accept all of our values. Yet it can make them free men and women in the area in which freedom is most important. We should be wary of an educational program which seeks to change or control student behavior on any other basis than rational self-determination, the basis that command of knowledge provides.

5. *Written tests are well suited to measure the student's command of useful knowledge.* All knowledge can be expressed in propositions. Propositions are statements that can be judged to be true or false. Scholars, scientists, research workers—all those concerned with adding to our store of knowledge—spend most of their time formulating and verifying propositions.

Implicit in every true-false or multiple-choice test item is a proposition, or several propositions. Essay tests also require a student to demonstrate his command of knowledge.

Some elements of novelty are essential in any question intended to test a student's command of knowledge. He should not be allowed to respond successfully on the basis of rote learning or verbal association. He should not be asked a stereotyped question to which a pat answer probably has been committed to memory.

6. *The classroom teacher should prepare most of the tests used to measure educational achievement in the classroom.* Many published tests are available for classroom use in measuring educational aptitude or achievement in broad areas of knowledge. But there are very

few which are specifically appropriate for measuring the achievement of the objectives of a particular unit of work or of a particular period of instruction. Publishers of textbooks sometimes supply booklets of test questions to accompany their texts. These can be useful, although all too often the test questions supplied are of inferior quality—hastily written, unreviewed, untested, and subject to correct response on the basis of rote learning as well as on the basis of understanding.

Even if good ready-made tests were generally available, a case could still be made for teacher-prepared tests; the chief reason being that the process of test development can help the teacher define his objectives. This process can result in tests that are more highly relevant than any external tests are likely to be. It can make the process of measuring educational achievement an integral part of the whole process of instruction, as it should be.

7. *To measure achievement effectively the classroom teacher must be (a) a master of the knowledge or skill to be tested, and (b) a master of the practical arts of testing.* No courses in educational measurement, no books or articles on the improvement of classroom tests, are likely to enable a poor teacher to make good tests. A teacher's command of the knowledge he is trying to teach, his understanding of common misconceptions regarding this content, his ability to invent novel questions and problems, and his ability to express these clearly and concisely; all these are crucial to his success in test construction. It is unfortunately true that some people who have certificates to teach lack one or more of these prerequisites to good teaching and good testing.

However, there are also some tricks of the trade of test construction. A course in educational measurement, or a book or article on classroom testing can teach these things. Such a course may also serve to shake a teacher's faith—constructively and wholesomely—in some of the popular misconceptions about the processes of testing educational achievement. Among these misconceptions are the belief that only essay tests are useful for measuring the development of a student's higher mental processes; that a test score should indicate what proportion a student does know of what he ought to know; that mistakes in scoring are the main source of error in test scores.

8. *The quality of a classroom test depends on the relevance of the tasks included in it, on the representativeness of its sampling of all aspects of instruction, and on the reliability of the scores it yields.* If a test question presents a problem like those the student may expect to encounter in his later life outside the classroom, and if the course in which his achievement is being tested did in fact try to teach him how to deal with such problems, then the question is relevant. If the test questions involve, in proportion to their importance, all aspects of achievement the course undertakes to develop, it samples representatively. If the scores students receive on a test agree closely with those they would receive on an independent, equivalent test, then the test yields reliable scores.

Relevance, representativeness and reliability are all matters of degree. Procedures and formulas for calculating estimates of test reliability are well developed, and are described in most books on educational measurement. Estimates of representativeness and relevance are more subjective, less quantitative. Yet this does not mean that relevance and representativeness are any less important than reliability. The more a test has of each the better. While it is possible to have an irrelevant and unrepresentative but highly reliable test, it is seldom necessary and never desirable, to sacrifice any one of the three for the others.

Either essay or objective test forms can be used to present relevant tasks to the examinees. Ordinarily, the greater the novelty of a test question, that is, the smaller the probability that the student has encountered the same question before, or been taught a pat answer to it, the greater its relevance. Because of the greater number of questions involved, it is sometimes easier to include a representative sample of tasks in an objective than in an essay test. For the same reason, and also because of greater uniformity in scoring, objective tests are likely to yield somewhat more reliable scores than are essay tests.

9. *The more variable the scores from a test designed to have a certain maximum possible score, the higher the expected reliability of those scores.* Reliability is sometimes defined as the proportion of the total variability among the test scores which is not attributable to errors of measurement. The size of the errors of measurement depends on the nature of the test—the kind and the number of items in it. Hence for a particular test, any increase in the total variability of the scores is likely to increase the proportion which is not due to errors of measurement, and hence to increase the reliability of the test.

Figure 1 shows some hypothetical score distributions for three tests. The essay test consists of 10 questions worth 10 points each, scored by a teacher who regards 75 as a passing score on such a test. The true-false test consists of 100 items, each of which is worth one point if correctly answered, with no subtraction for wrong answers. The multiple-choice test also includes 100 items, each of which offers four alternative answer options. It, too, is scored only for the number of correct answers given, with no "correction for guessing."

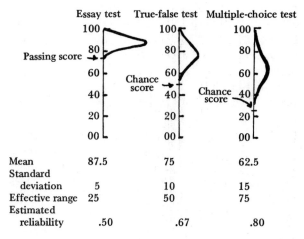

	Essay test	True-false test	Multiple-choice test
Mean	87.5	75	62.5
Standard deviation	5	10	15
Effective range	25	50	75
Estimated reliability	.50	.67	.80

Figure 1. Hypothetical score distributions for three tests.

Note, in the data at the bottom of Figure 1, the differences among the tests in average score (mean), in variability (standard deviation), in effective range and in estimated reliability. While these are hypothetical data, derived from calculations based on certain assumptions, they are probably reasonably representative of the results most teachers achieve in using tests of these types.

It is possible to obtain scores whose reliability is above .90 using 100 multiple-choice items, but it is not easy to do, and classroom teachers seldom do it in the tests they construct. It is also possible to handle 100-point essay tests and 100-item true-false tests so that their reliability will equal that of a 100-item multiple-choice test. But again, it is not easy to do and classroom teachers seldom succeed in doing it.

10. *The reliability of a test can be increased by increasing the number of questions (or independent points to be scored) and by sharpening the power of individual questions to discriminate between students of high and low achievement.* Figure 2 illustrates the increases of test reliability which can be expected as a result of increasing the number of items (or independent points to be scored) in a test. Doubling the length of a

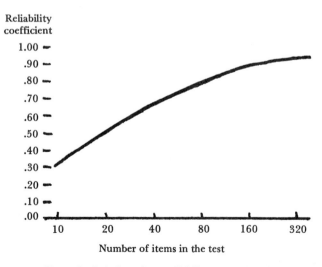

Figure 2. Relation of test reliability to test length.

10-item test whose reliability coefficient is .33 increases the reliability to .50. Doubling again brings it up to .67, and so on. These estimates are based on the Spearman-Brown formula for predicting the reliability of a lengthened test. While the formula requires assumptions which may not be justified in all cases, its predictions are usually quite accurate.

Figure 3 shows how the maximum discriminating power of an item is related to its level of difficulty. These discrimination indices are simply differences between the proportions of correct response from good and poor students. Good students are those whose total test scores fall among the top 27 per cent of the students tested. Poor students are those whose scores make up the bottom 27 per cent. An item of 50 per cent difficulty does not necessarily have (and usually will not have) an index of discrimination of 1.00. Its discriminating power may be zero, or even negative. But items of middle difficulty have higher ceilings on their discriminating power. What is more important, they not

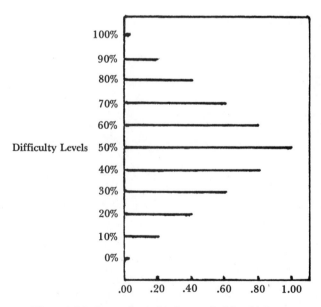

Figure 3. Maximum discrimination attainable with items at different levels of difficulty.

only can have, but usually do have, greater discriminating power than very easy or very difficult items. An item that no one answers correctly, or that everyone answers correctly, cannot discriminate at all. Such an item adds nothing to the reliability of a test.

In summary, the 10 principles stated and discussed in this article represent only a sample of the important things classroom teachers need to know about educational measurement. These principles, and the brief discussion of each presented here, may serve to call into question some common practices in classroom testing, or to suggest some ways in which classroom tests might be improved. They are not likely, and are not intended, to say all that needs to be said or do all that needs to be done to improve educational measurement in the classroom. It is our sincere belief, however, that a teacher whose classroom testing reflects an understanding of these principles will do a better than average job of measuring student achievement.

8. Making the Classroom Test: A Guide for Teachers

Educational Testing Service

All teachers have to make tests. But making good tests is not easy. The purpose of this pamphlet is to offer practical suggestions which may help you to make better tests.

To make a good test, you should have clearly in mind what you are testing for and how you plan to use the results. A carefully planned unit of study deserves a carefully planned test covering the unit. As you know, good tests are not made by merely "throwing together" questions more or less related to the work you have been teaching until you have written enough to keep the pupils busy for a class period. A test prepared in a haphazard manner will not *really* tell you how much your pupils have learned. Furthermore, it may well leave your pupils confused about what they are supposed to have learned.

Let us consider the plans and procedures used by four teachers in making good tests. Their efforts illustrate basic general principles for constructing tests to meet specific classroom needs. First, the forethoughts and procedures of each teacher will be described. Then the general rules will be stated.

An Objective Achievement Test on Fifth-Grade Arithmetic

It was near the end of the school year and Mrs. Jackson, fifth-grade teacher, decided to give her pupils an arithmetic test covering the year's work. Her first step was to list the kinds of information she hoped to get from the test. She decided that, most of all, she wanted to get a general picture of class achievement with some indication of over-all areas of strength and weakness. Secondary purposes she listed were (1) to identify those pupils who might be especially weak in a particular arithmetic skill and (2) to measure the relative abilities of her students for purposes of report-card grading.

In trying to get an accurate picture of over-all class achievement, she decided that there were two ways in which she could classify the year's work: one was according to *the kind of computation required,* and the other was according to *the way the problem was presented.*

The kinds of computation required were

1. Multiplication
2. Division
3. Addition and Subtraction of Fractions
4. Measuring (distance, time, weight, temperature, etc.)
5. Decimals

The ways the problems were presented were

1. Simple computation, such as $21\overline{)\$1.05}$ or $1/2 + 1/3$
2. Problems requiring use of procedures learned previously, such as

   John missed 1/5 of the twenty words on a spelling test. How many words did he miss?

   or

   A group of twenty-nine children were making programs for a school assembly. They needed 435 programs. How many did each child have to make?

3. Problems requiring original thinking by pupils and use of "number sense." In these problems the pupils could not depend on previously learned procedures for a method of solution but must develop their own procedures for solution. Two problems of this type follow:

Problem one. Explain how you, as a fifth-grade pupil, using ten blocks, could prove to a fourth-grade pupil that 1/2 is bigger than 2/5.

Problem two. You are standing directly in front of Building A and looking off at building B in the distance. Here is the way the two buildings look to you:

Building A

Building B

The rooms in both buildings are the same height. By looking at the windows, decide which of the following is true:

(A) Both buildings are the same height.
(B) Building A is two-thirds as high as Building B.
(C) Building A is one and one-third times as high as Building B.
(D) Building A is twice as high as building B.
(E) You can't tell from looking at the buildings which one is higher.

    (Answer: B)

Using these two ways for classifying the questions (according to the kind of computation required and according to the way the problem was presented), Mrs. Jackson was now ready to make *a written plan* for the test. She intended that this plan would provide for a test *paralleling* the emphasis given to various points in class.

Mrs. Jackson wrote out her test plan in the form of a "two-way grid." In a two-way grid each question is classified in two dimensions.

The two-way grid that Mrs. Jackson made for the arithmetic test is on page 6. Since she planned to allow an hour for the test, she thought 40 questions would be about the right number. The numbers in the boxes represent questions—these questions to be of a type described by the two dimensions of the grid.

Way Problem Presented

Kind of Computation Required	Routine Computation	Thought Problems Following Procedures Taught Previously	Thought Problems Requiring Students to Develop New Procedures
Fractions	7	4	1
Multiplication	2	3	1
Division	3	4	1
Measuring	1	5	1
Decimals	3	3	1

After Mrs. Jackson completed the two-way grid, she found it relatively easy to write most of the questions for the test. She was able to write many questions by paralleling questions from the arithmetic textbook itself. However, she found it quite challenging to write the five problems which would require students to develop new procedures.

Mrs. Jackson believed that the test covered understandings and skills in which her pupils had been well prepared. Therefore, she expected the very best students to get all or nearly all of the questions right, and she expected even the below-average students to get a majority of the questions right. She did not, however, make the mistake of deciding in advance that some minimum score—say 28 questions right (70%)—would represent a passing mark. She knew from previous experience that sometimes her questions turned out to be more difficult than they first seemed to her. She decided to wait until she could look at the scores actually made on the whole test and could scrutinize carefully any questions which proved particularly troublesome.

As it happened, most of the students did well on the test, although no one had a perfect paper. On the basis of the test, Mrs. Jackson felt that her class had achieved the objectives of the work in arithmetic. She did notice, however, that a number of students had difficulty with the problems involving decimals. Therefore she decided to spend more time working on decimals in the few weeks remaining in the school year. And then there was one student who failed all the division problems, although he did fairly well on the rest of the test. She arranged to give this student special help in division.

Most of the students had between 30 and 35 questions right. However, there were a few who scored above, and a few who fell below this middle range. Knowing which students were in the middle and which were above or below was useful to Mrs. Jackson in assigning report-card grades. Of course she also took into account each pupil's class work and his standing on other tests.

In evaluating her test, Mrs. Jackson felt it had been reasonably successful in meeting the purposes for which she had planned it. The test had given her a good picture of over-all class achievement and it had pointed up the weakness in decimals. It had not been planned to be highly diagnostic, but it had helped to identify one pupil who was especially weak in division. In addition, although the test did not rank all of her students in the exact order of their arithmetic abilities, it had given her information that was useful for grading purposes.

An Essay Test to Measure a Special Ability in Eighth-Grade American History

Mr. Frank's eighth-grade American history class had been studying the fighting that took place between the Indians and the settlers in the western states. The class had just completed several discussions on the rights of each side.

The major purpose of having these discussions was to improve the pupils' ability to find and express convincingly facts and arguments in support of their opinions.

Mr. Frank decided that he would like to give a test to measure his class's skill in this ability. At first, he considered giving an objective test. He thought he might list a number of arguments presented by both the Indians and the settlers and then ask the class to identify those which were backed up by facts. But then he decided against using this kind of test. An objective test would require the student to select sound arguments: it would not call upon him to develop and present them convincingly as he would do in actual discussion. Accordingly, Mr. Frank decided that an essay test would satisfy his purposes best.

Since the subject matter of the test was limited, it was unnecessary for Mr. Frank to prepare a written plan for the test. In a sense, the test questions constituted the test plan. Here is the test he prepared. It had three questions:

1. Pretend that you are a settler and give three general reasons why you think your side is right in the war with the Indians. For each of the reasons, describe an actual happening to support your argument.
2. Pretend that you are an Indian and give three reasons why you think your side is right in the war with the settlers. For each of the reasons, describe an actual happening to support your argument.
3. Look at the six reasons given by both sides and decide which one would be most dangerous if everyone accepted this kind of reasoning. Give two examples of how people might do bad things if they accepted this kind of reasoning.

Before scoring the papers, Mr. Frank analyzed the points which he thought would appear in an ideal response and decided how much he would count for each point. He decided not to take off credit for mistakes in spelling and English usage. But he planned to show the English teacher any paper which was especially poorly written so that the English teacher might give help in composition writing to those pupils who needed it.

After Mr. Frank corrected the papers, he found that most of the pupils had proceeded well on Questions 1 and 2 requiring reasons and examples. However, many of them had floundered on Question 3, which required them to point out the dangerous implications of one argument. Because of their difficulty with Question 3, Mr. Frank decided to organize a series of classroom debates, so that the students would get practice in extending, attacking, and defending an argument.

On an essay test of this sort, scores are not highly reliable. On a second reading, after a little time lapse, Mr. Frank would find it difficult to give every paper the same mark as on the first reading. Furthermore, several teachers grading the same papers would probably not agree very closely with one another. Therefore, Mr. Frank avoided giving an exact numerical score for each paper but instead assigned three general grades: good, average, and poor. However, he wrote many comments on the papers so that the pupils would have a better idea of the strengths and weaknesses of their arguments. He also read several papers to the class for discussion purposes, making full use of the test as an instructional device.

A Tenth-Grade Biology Test Especially Designed to Rank Students in Order of Ability

The students in Mr. Orlando's tenth-grade biology class were all in the college-preparatory curriculum. Moreover, they were all good science students who had been especially selected for accelerated work.

Although it was unlikely that any of these students would fail, Mr. Orlando wanted to find out who were the "A" students, who were the "B" students, and who, if any, should be given "C's." He also wanted to select three students for scholarships to attend a special summer science institute at the state university.

To get a highly reliable ranking of his students on their knowledge and understanding of important topics in biology, Mr. Orlando decided to give a *series* of tests on the various subjects covered in the course. The first test he planned was on a reading assignment about antibodies.

He knew from previous experience in testing this class that, if his questions generally paralleled the entire reading assignment, most of the class would answer them correctly. Such questions would not help him much to rank the students in precise order or to select the three scholarship winners. Therefore, he decided to focus this test on "critical points" in the reading assignment. That is, the test questions would be on the parts of the reading assignment which were hard to grasp and yet were important for complete understanding. These questions would have to be so difficult that average or even good students might well miss them, but the very best students would probably get many of them right. At the same time, Mr. Orlando was very careful to avoid questions which might be difficult simply because they were on trivial details.

He divided the reading assignment into four important content areas. Then, within each of the content areas, he planned to test for two skills which he considered *crucial* for top-flight science students. The four content areas and the two skills within these areas, as well as the number of questions, are presented in the grid below:

Skills: Content:	Questions Requiring Exact Definition of Technical Terms	Questions Requiring Application of Information from Reading Assignment
The Antigen-Antibody Reaction	3	10
The Rhesus Blood Factor	3	10
The A, B, and O Blood Types	3	10
The Importance of Antibodies in Disease	1	10

Although Mr. Orlando intended to use objective questions for measuring skill in defining technical terms, he at first thought that he would need to use essay questions for measuring skill in applying information. In fact, he had already written the following question for the test:

> You are given two test tubes, one labeled Protein Q, the other labeled Protein Z. How could you tell if these tubes really contained different proteins? Outline the experimental procedure you would follow.

However, to answer this question would take many of the students at least ten minutes. It might take some of the better students even longer because they would tend to describe the experiment in greater detail than the others. At this rate, it would take most of the students the better part of the day to finish the test.

Therefore, Mr. Orlando began to consider the possibility of using objective questions instead. He rewrote the essay question, above, in this way:

> You are given two test tubes, one labeled Protein Q, the other labeled Protein Z. Which of the following would be the best *first step* to find out if these tubes really contain different proteins?
>
> (A) Inject a rabbit with either Protein Q or Protein Z.
> (B) Mix Proteins Q and Z together to see whether a precipitate is formed.
> (C) Take blood from a rabbit and centrifuge out the red blood cells.
> (D) Add a serum to either Protein Q or Protein Z.
> (E) Inject a rabbit with a combination of Protein Q and Protein Z.
>
> (Answer: A)

To answer this question would require most students only a minute or two. Of course, the objective question above requires simply selection of the *first step* in the experiment, while the essay question would require a *complete description* of it. Yet Mr. Orlando felt that most of those who could select the first step correctly would also be able to carry through the whole experiment. And by using the objective question, Mr. Orlando was now able to ask many more questions than if he had used the essay type.

Here are some other questions he wrote. The first two require an exact understanding of some of the technical vocabulary in the reading assignment. The others require application of information given in the reading assignment.

1. An antigen is
   (A) the opposite of an antibody
   (B) the residue of an antibody
   (C) the stimulus for antibody formation
   (D) the result of antibody formation
   (E) the same as an antibody
      (Answer: C)

2. The antibodies in passive immunity are
   (A) created by the recipient
   (B) preformed
   (C) created by fresh exposure
   (D) self-reproducing
   (E) created by antitoxins
      (Answer: B)

   In the following table fill in the possible blood groups of fathers.

   Blood Types Determining Possible Parentage of a Child, Making Use of the A and B Proteins Only

	Known Blood Group of Mother	Blood Group of Child	Possible Blood Groups of Father
3.	A	A	
4.	O	A	
5.	B	AB	
6.	B	A	

   (Answers: 3-A, B, AB, O; 4-A, AB; 5-A, AB; 6-A, AB.)

7. A male child is born with erythroblastosis fetalis which requires a blood exchange. Which one of the following must be true?
   (A) The mother was Rh+ and the father was Rh−.
   (B) The mother was Rh− and the father was Rh+.
   (C) The mother was B+ and the father was A−:'
   (D) The mother had B type blood and the father had A type.
   (E) The mother had O type blood and the father had AB type.
      (Answer: B)

8. Which of the following is NOT an immunological approach to combating disease?
   (A) Salk vaccine
   (B) Gamma globulin
   (C) Penicillin injection
   (D) Tetanus toxoid
   (E) Smallpox vaccination
      (Answer: C)

The class found the test challenging and enjoyed going over the questions with Mr. Orlando afterwards. Although there were a few questions that most of the students got right and a few that practically everyone got wrong, most of the questions were missed by about half the students. The average score in the class was 23 out of the 50 right. The lowest score was 9 right and the top score was 48 right. The test helped Mr. Orlando to rank the studetns with some confidence. He felt that the test also helped demonstrate to the class the kind of reasoning-from-data required for advanced work in science.

A Twelfth-Grade English Test for Diagnosing Common Errors in Usage and Spelling

It was the beginning of the school year and Miss Barstow had been assigned a special twelfth-grade class in remedial English. All the pupils in her class had done poorly in high-school English. The English Department had decided that these pupils should be drilled intensively to improve their basic skills in composition writing before graduation from high school.

Miss Barstow decided that she needed to use a diagnostic test to find out areas of strength and weakness for each pupil.

The English Department had already designated six basic types of error in composition writing to be corrected in this class. These were:

1. Run-together sentences, or the comma-splice:
   "It is snowing very hard today, the children will probably go sleigh riding tomorrow."

2. Incomplete sentences:
   "When the boat struck the rock and the water poured in and the sailors climbed up into the rigging."
3. Misspelling of common everyday words:
   "You should recieve an answer tomorrow."
4. Disagreement between subject and verb:
   "When they was told what to do, they did it."
5. Confusion as to the case of pronouns:
   "The man refused to tell either Harry or I where the money was hidden."
6. Use of unacceptable colloquial expressions:
   "He could of won the race if he had tried harder."

The purpose of Miss Barstow's test was to find out to what extent *each of her students* was likely to make *each kind of mistake* listed below.

To get an accurate picture for individual diagnosis, Miss Barstow realized that she needed a fairly long test. She wrote 20 items for each of the 6 kinds of error—a total of 120 items. Then she wrote 30 sentences that had no errors at all. She now had a total of 150 items in the test. She put all these items in random order and left enough space between them for the students to write in the necessary corrections. She told the students that, although 30 of the sentences were correct, each of the others contained a common error in either spelling, usage, or grammar. Then she allowed the students 2 fifty-minute periods to make whatever changes they thought necessary to correct the sentences.

After the students had finished the test, Miss Barstow divided the sentences into the types of error they represented and then scored each group of 20 sentences separately. Thus she had six scores for every student, one for each of the six kinds of error. The 30 correct sentences were not included in the scoring. Their function was to make it a bit more difficult for the students to identify the errors.

Using the test results, Miss Barstow was able to plan remedial work for each student's specific weaknesses.

Basic Rules of Test-Making Illustrated by the Four Tests

You have now read how four teachers tackled the problem of making tests. From their experiences you can see that there are basic rules which should almost always be followed:

1. Have the purpose of your test clearly in mind. To what extent are you trying to measure how well your students have learned a particular unit of study? To what extent do you hope to rank your students accurately according to their abilities? How highly diagnostic of the strengths and weaknesses of individual pupils do you want your test to be?

2. Make a careful plan for the test questions. Unless your test covers a very limited unit of work, the plan should be *written*. Most plans for tests are not so simple that they can be kept firmly in mind. Furthermore, when you examine the written plan, you are better able to recognize its strengths and weaknesses.

3. If your test is mainly diagnostic in a basic skill area (as was Miss Barstow's English test), you should prepare at least 10 questions—*preferably more*—for each sub-test that you use. These sub-tests should yield separate scores on the various elements needed for mastery of the skill.

4. If you are trying to find out how well your class has mastered a particular unit of study (as was Mrs. Jackson in her fifth-grade arithmetic test), you should make a test which parallels the work in class. Generally speaking, this test should not be too difficult and the commonly accepted figure of seventy per cent for a passing score is probably appropriate for many classes.

5. When the major purpose of your test is to rank a selected group of students in order of their achievement (as was the purpose of Mr. Orlando's biology test), the questions should be on "critical" points of learning. These are the points that go beyond the superficial and obvious. They are "critical" in the sense that it is necessary to understand them for truly

high-level achievement. Questions on "critical" points often require understanding implications, applying information, and reorganizing data.

For if questions are asked only on material which has been specifically taught in class and which has merely to be remembered, scores are apt to bunch near the top of the range and will not help much in determining an accurate rank order of achievement. For ranking purposes such as Mr. Orlando's, questions should go beyond what has been memorized and ask the student to use his knowledge in new situations for which it is suitable. Generally, the most accurate ranking will be achieved by making all the questions of medium difficulty for the group. But when a major purpose is to select a few of the very best students, items should be more difficult. However, do not write questions on inconsequential details just to catch students. Instead, focus on important understandings that you think the better students should have—the kinds of understandings you would not expect of poorer students. Then, even the best students are likely to miss a few questions, but their total scores will give a good estimate of their relative standings.

Special Problems in Writing and Scoring Tests

After you have decided on the purposes of the test and have made a written plan to fit these purposes, you will want to consider the following special problems about making tests and scoring them.

When Should Essay Questions Be Used and When Objective?

There are no categorical rules to tell you which type of question to use. However, it will be helpful to keep clearly in mind the characteristics of each type. Then you will be able to decide which will be most suitable for the particular purpose and circumstances of the test you are making.

The summary on page 16 compares a few of the major characteristics of the two types.

	ESSAY	OBJECTIVE
Abilities Measured	Requires the student to express himself in his own words, using information from his own background and knowledge.	Requires the student to select correct answers from given options, or to supply an answer limited to one word or phrase.
	Can tap high levels of reasoning such as required in inference, organization of ideas, comparison and contrast.	Can *also* tap high levels of reasoning such as required in inference, organization of ideas, comparison and contrast.
	Does *not* measure purely factual information efficiently.	Measures knowledge of facts efficiently.
Scope	Covers only a limited field of knowledge in any one test. Essay questions take so long to answer that relatively few can be answered in a given period of time. Also, the student who is especially fluent can often avoid discussing points of which he is unsure.	Covers a broad field of knowledge in one test. Since objective questions may be answered quickly, one test may contain many questions. A broad coverage helps provide reliable measurement.
Incentive to Pupils	Encourages pupils to learn how to organize their own ideas and express them effectively.	Encourages pupils to build up a broad background of knowledge and abilities.
Ease of Preparation	Requires writing only a few questions for a test. Tasks must be clearly defined, general enough to offer some leeway, specific enough to set limits.	Requires writing many questions for a test. Wording must avoid ambiguities and "give-aways." Distractors should embody most likely misconceptions.
Scoring	Usually very time-consuming to score.	Can be scored quickly.
	Permits teachers to comment directly on the reasoning processes of individual pupils. However, an answer may be scored differently by different teachers or by the same teacher at different times.	Answer generally scored only right or wrong but scoring is very accurate and consistent.

How Can You Learn to Write Better Objective Questions?

A common problem is how to write objective questions that tap complex abilities. First, you need to define the kind of behavior which seems to demonstrate the ability you are trying to measure. Then ask, "How can I make up questions that will elicit this kind of behavior?"

In order to get ideas for writing your own test questions, you will find it useful to look over the questions used in published tests. You may be surprised at the ingenuity of the professional test-writer in constructing questions which measure high-level abilities.

Objective questions, generally speaking, are classified into four major types: (1) Multiple-choice, (2) Matching, (3) Completion or Fill-in, (4) True-False. There are numerous variations among these types. These have been described at length in articles on measurement and in measurement textbooks (for a bibliography see page 27).

The following samples not only illustrate the four general types of objective questions, but also offer further examples of how objective questions can be constructed to require not just memorization of facts but applications of learnings and skills to new situations.

Multiple-choice*

1. Tom wanted to find what effect fertilizer has on garden plants. He put some good soil in garden boxes. To Box A he added fertilizer containing a large amount of nitrogen. To Box B he added fertilizer containing a large amount of phosphorus. In each box he planted twelve bean seeds. He watered each box with the same amount of water. One thing missing from Tom's experiment was a box of soil with
   (A) both fertilizers added
   (B) neither nitrogen nor phosphorus added

---

*Items 1–4 by permission of the Cooperative Test Division, Educational Testing Service.

(C) several kinds of seeds planted

(D) no seeds planted

(Answer: B)

2. "Many young people of today are taking a great interest in the magazine *Suburbia*. It is of a fairly large size and of a considerable number of pages." In the second sentence above how could the size of the magazine be indicated most effectively?

(A) By comparing it with one or two well-known magazines

(B) By giving length, width, thickness, weight, and number of pages

(C) By drawing a scale model

(D) By telling how many articles each issue contains

(Answer: A)

By permission Army Times Publishing Company

3. The cartoon illustrates which of the following characteristics of the party system in the United States?
   (A) Strong party discipline is often lacking.
   (B) The parties are responsive to the will of the voters.
   (C) The parties are often more concerned with politics than with the national welfare.
   (D) Bipartisanship often exists in name only.

   (Answer: A)

4. The situation shown in the cartoon is *least* likely to occur at which of the following times?
   (A) During the first session of a new Congress
   (B) During a political party convention
   (C) During a primary election campaign
   (D) During a presidential election campaign

   (Answer: D)

Matching

Read the statements below, carefully paying attention to their relation to one another. Then next to each statement mark A, B, C, or D as indicated.

   (A) If the statement contains the *central* idea around which most of the statements can be grouped.
   (B) If the statement contains a main *supporting* idea of the central idea.
   (C) If the statement contains an *illustrative* fact or detailed statement related to a main supporting idea.
   (D) If the statement contains an idea or ideas which are *irrelevant*.

1. The Roman roads connected all parts of the Empire with Rome.
2. The Roman roads were so well built that some of them remain today.
3. One of the greatest achievements of the Romans was their extensive and durable system of roads.
4. Wealthy travelers in Roman times used horse-drawn coaches.

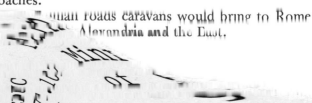

mall roads caravans would bring to Rome
Alexandria and the Dust,

6. In present-day Italy some of the roads used are original Roman roads.

(Answers: 1-B, 2-B, 3-A, 4-D, 5-C, 6-C)

Completion or Fill-in

In the blank of each sentence write the word or number which best completes the sentence.

1. If people's eyes were not sensitive to blue light, objects which now appear blue would appear . . . .

(Answer: black)

2. A game was played in which 28 people participated. The average final score was exactly 78. If 21 people had scores of less than 78 and 7 people had scores of more than 78 and if only whole-number scores were given, then the highest score must have been *at least* . . . .

(answer: 81)

True-False

In the space at the left mark whether the statement is true or false. Mark plus for true and zero for false.

. . . . .1. If the Cascade Mountains were 500 miles farther east, western Oregon would have an increased rainfall. (Answer: +)

. . . . .2. There is no point inside a circle farther from the edge of the circle than the length of the radius of the circle. (Answer: +)

How to avoid certain pitfalls in writing objective questions is given extensive treatment in the literature on test writing. For example, in multiple-choice or matching items, the item writer is advised to make all the choices plausible to one who does not know the correct answer. He is also advised to avoid the use of so-called "specific determiners." Examples of "specific determiners" are terms of extremes such as "always," "never," "all." A test-wise student can often guess correctly that a statement using one of these words is false. On the other hand, an extraordinarily detailed or qualified statement—to make extreme terms hold true—may also be a "specific determiner."

Two other obvious pitfalls you need to avoid in writing test questions should also be mentioned:

Reading Difficulty

Unless you are trying to test reading ability, write your questions in language that is easy for your pupils to understand.

EXAMPLE

Poor   If a man makes a business transaction wherein he purchases a motor vehicle for one thousand five hundred and twenty-five dollars and at a later date sells said vehicle in another business transaction for one thousand two hundred and sixty dollars, what is his net loss?

Better A man buys a car for $1525 and sells it later for $1260. What is the difference between the purchase price and the selling price? (Answer: $265)

Ambiguities

Always state your questions so that there can be only one interpretation.

EXAMPLES

Poor   The shortest day of the year is in
(A) March (B) June (C) September (D) December

Better The shortest day of the year in the northern hemisphere is in
(A) March (B) June (C) September (D) December
(Answer: D)

Poor   Which of the following books can be called humorous?
(A) *A Christmas Carol*
(B) *Tom Sawyer*

(C) *Treasure Island*
(D) *Silas Marner*

(The student might think he is expected to select more than one of the options because several of the books contain humorous incidents.)

Better   Which one of the following books is most humorous?
(A) *A Christmas Carol*
(B) *Tom Sawyer*
(C) *Treasure Island*
(D) *Silas Marner*

(Answer: B)

Some of the sources cited in the Bibliography provide numerous examples and detailed discussion of defective test items. Many of the stock admonitions appear self-evident. Yet if every item is not systematically checked, defects that later seem obvious to you may sneak by. Fortunately, you need not "go it alone" in trying to produce good questions. You will find it very helpful to work with another teacher or even a group of teachers in reviewing each other's questions. It is often surprising how easy it is to find weaknesses in questions written by someone else, and yet overlook the very same weaknesses in your own questions.

You will also find your own students are excellent critics. If you go over the questions wtih your students after the test, they are usually more than willing to point out ambiguities in phrasing, falseness in the keyed answer, or any other flaws.

How Can You Improve Reliability in Scoring Essay Questions?

To begin with, you should state the question in enough detail so that your pupils understand what is expected. Otherwise many of them will discuss quite different aspects of a question and their answers will vary greatly in length, points covered, and general approach. Under these conditions, you will find it difficult to compare the quality of the different answers and assign grades accurately.

Below is an example of an essay question which is too general, followed by an example of one which is stated in greater detail:

EXAMPLE

Poor   Explain why you think the Uniter Nations has been a success or a failure.

Better An important function of the United Nations is to help settle disputes between nations. Describe how one dispute was handled successfully, pointing out how the settlement illustrates a general strength of the United Nations. Describe also how one dispute was handled unsuccessfully, pointing out how this illustrates a general weakness of the United Nations. Your essay should be about 300-400 words in length (2 or 3 pages in longhand).

Various systematic procedures have been set up to make the scoring of essay questions more reliable. These procedures are useful but, unfortunately, time-consuming. You will have to decide how conscientiously you wish to follow these procedures—whether the increase in reliability is worth the additional time and effort.

The following method for scoring essay questions is described by Graham.* It is clear cut and relatively simple. You may find it useful.

(1) The teacher *analyzes the points* that he thinks should be made in the ideal response *and assigns a numerical weight* to each point. Some points may be of greater importance; hence, they would be weighted appropriately. The instructor may wish to allow extra credit for clear organization of thinking. Sometimes he may feel that he cannot develop a "scoring key" until he reads a cross-section of students' papers. Whether derived by teacher-analysis, or by analysis of pupil responses, or by a combination of the two approaches, a systematic method of scoring using numerical values or percentages increases objectivity. (2) The test reader *evaluates all the responses to one question* before going on to score the next question. (3) As the teacher reads, he *tosses the papers into five piles* (high to low in quality). This procedure may be unnecessary if the instructor is satisfied with the quantitative

---

*See Bibliography (7)

appraisal described in (1) above; but if he also wants a qualitative estimate, he may need to re-check his classifications to determine if the papers in each pile are indeed of similar quality. (4) *Anonymity is necessary* for the accurate scoring of essay tests because of the ubiquitous "halo effect." The easiest way to prevent this kind of subjectivity is to ask pupils to write their names *only* on the back of their test papers.

Since it is difficult to grade essays reliably, you will usually be more concerned with writing comments than awarding grades. Your written comment on a paper will help the student more than a grade in understanding his strengths and weaknesses. However, if essay tests must be used for grades, reliability can be increased by basing the final grade on several essay tests rather than one.

What Kind of Statistical Analysis of Test Questions Should the Teacher Make?

The very word "statistics" causes some teachers to shudder and feel lost. This need not be. Practical statistics can be quite simple. Of course few teachers are willing to spend time on statistical analysis of a question that is not to be used again. However, many teachers are well aware of the advantages of a copious stockpile of questions. If certain characteristics of these questions are known, it is possible to design a test more effectively for a specific purpose and group.

Two simplified procedures by which teachers can obtain such information about their test items have been described in detail in two publications listed in the Bibliography. Diederich (4) urges pupil participation in the analysis of test items, emphasizing instructional values. Katz (8) shows how the classroom teacher can complete an item analysis in remarkably little time. In general, item analysis tells you two things that you will want to know about the questions you are keeping in your stockpile: (1) how difficult each question is; (2) how well each question discriminates between high- and low-ranking students on the test as a whole.

Difficulty

A simple measure of difficulty is the per cent of students who got the question right on any one test. For example, the first time you use a particular question, 75 per cent of the students may get it right. If you keep a card file of your questions, then on the back of the card for this question you write the date and "75% right." You make a similar entry every time you use the question. Then, knowing in advance the probable difficulty of the questions, you will be able to "tailor" your test (in a style determined by your purpose) to fit the ability level of your class.

As the basic rules (pages 14-15) pointed out, when you want to see whether your class has mastered a fundamental unit of study, questions will tend to be easy. But when the principal purpose of the test is to rank all the students in the group in order of ability—for example, to give them grades which reflect standing in class—try to use questions which are of middle difficulty.* If you want to discriminate more precisely among the better students (as Mr. Orlando did), all of the questions should be of greater difficulty. In fact, test-makers speak of "peaking a test at the cut-off point"—that is, trying to make each test item so difficult that (on a free response test) only about 50% of the lowest pupils selected or highest pupils rejected will answer it correctly.

Of course, in writing difficult questions, you will take care that the difficulty is based on significant parts of the classwork, which your better students should be able to understand. As has already been emphasized, the difficulty should not be based on memorization of trivial details or result from tricky or ambiguous wording. In other words, your questions should be fair and truly representative of important teaching objectives. Very often questions that require pupils to apply information learned in the classroom to new situations are good for this purpose. The science test that Mr. Orlando made for his biology class included many questions of this type.

---

*Ideally, for this purpose, each question on a free-response test should be so difficult that only 50% of the group get it right; on a 5-option multiple-choice test, 60%; 4-option multiple-choice, 62%; 3-option, 66%; true-false, 75%—assuming that the score is the number of items answered correctly.

In connection with difficulty, most tests should give your students sufficient time to consider each question and answer it to the best of their abilities. Probably about 90 per cent of the students should complete all the questions on a test. Of course, if your purpose is to test speed itself, then you will expect fewer students to finish the test. For example, if you were testing speed of reading, you might expect only 10 or 15 per cent to answer all the questions.

Discrimination

You will want to know how effectively each question contributes to the discrimination between the high-scoring and low-scoring pupils on the test as a whole. If an important purpose of your test is to rank students according to ability, some questions will help more than others. The discriminating power of each question can be estimated by these steps:

1. Arrange the test papers in order of scores, with the highest score on top.
2. Take a specified quantity (ten are easy to handle) of the papers from the top and the same quantity from the bottom. Place them in separate piles called High and Low, respectively.
3. Now you are ready to analyze the individual questions. For each question count the number of Highs who got it right and the number of Lows who got it right.
4. Convert these numbers to per cents. If the question is a good one for ranking students, then substantially more of the Highs than Lows will have answered it correctly.

For example, assume there are 10 students in the top group and 10 in the bottom group. On the first question, 8 of the Highs (80%) but only 3 of the Lows (30%) got the right answer. This is a good question for ranking students because it is clear that the students who generally did well on the test were able to get the question right, while those who did poorly on the test as a whole tended to get it wrong. The per cent of the top group and the per cent of the bottom group getting the item right may be written on the back of the question card in your stockpile of items. In the example given above you would note H = 80%, L = 30%. Later you may refer to this information in assembling a test which will be especially effective in discrimination.

You will want to take a close and suspicious "second look" at any question where the top students had as much difficulty as the poorer students—or more. Possibly the question is not so clearly stated as it should be. If it is a multiple-choice item, perhaps one of the "wrong" options is too close to being correct. Look over each question where the results of the analysis indicate the possibility of a flaw in the question and decide whether you can improve the question by rewriting.

When Should You Use a Published Test and When Should You Make Your Own?

If a published achievement test *covers the points* you wish to measure, you may use it instead of making your own test. Sometimes, however, it is impossible to find a published test that matches what you want to measure—particularly if you want a test covering a single unit of study. Thus, when you need a test covering only a few weeks of class work, you will ordinarily make your own. One important benefit from preparing your own test is that the very process of writing questions forces you to define your own teaching objectives in terms of specific skills and understandings.

However, there are many times when you may decide to use a published test. And, of course, your school probably gives standardized tests as part of its testing program. These tests offer several advantages. They have been written by specialists so that the general quality of questions is high. They have been subjected to careful statistical analysis so that the questions are controlled for difficulty and discrimination. They are accompanied by norms so that you are able to compare the performance of your pupils with the performance of a representative sample with known characteristics.

And finally, the fact that well-constructed achievement tests have been prepared by groups of experienced teachers, whose competence is generally recognized, gives you a check on your judgment of what should be measured. Their consensus on skills and understandings to be covered is not necessarily better than yours. But if it is substantially different from yours, it provides a valuable supplement to your estimates of student achievement in any area. It gives some notion of how well your pupils can do on a test of learnings that teachers in general may consider important.

A Word in Closing

The most scrupulous heed for all the cautions, admonitions, principles and procedures discussed in this pamphlet will not guarantee that you will make good tests—although it may do much to prevent bad ones. Good tests cannot be written merely by following any set of "rules." There is an art to good test-writing which involves elements of originality and creativity as well as knowledge of theory. This pamphlet does not pretend to provide competence in all elements of the art. Such competence seems to thrive on practice, criticism, tryout, analysis, and more practice.

However, this pamphlet does attempt to foster an attitude and approach which have helped many teachers to improve their tests. It has presented some essential principles and some realistic illustrations to serve as guides and touchstones in your efforts to make better classroom tests.

Bibliography

1. Anderson, Scarvia B., Katz, M. R., and Shimberg,B. *Meeting the Test.* New York: Scholastic Book Services, 1963.
2. Baron, D. and Bernard, H. W. *Evaluation Techniques for Classroom Teachers.* New York: McGraw-Hill, 1958. Chapter 12.
3. Bean, K. L. *Construction of Educational and Personnel Tests.* New York: McGraw-Hill, 1953.
4. Diederich, P. *Short-cut Statistics for Teacher-made Tests.* Evaluation and Advisory Service Series, No. 5. Princeton: Educational Testing Service, 1960.
5. Ebel, R. L. "Writing the Test Item." In E. F. Lindquist (Ed.), *Educational Measurement.* Washington, D. C.: American Council on Education, 1951. Chapter 7.

6. Furst, E. J. *Constructing Evaluation Instruments*. New York: Longmans, Green and Co., 1958.

7. Graham, Grace. "Teachers Can Construct Better Achievement Tests." *Curriculum Bulletin*. University of Oregon, Vol. XII, No. 170, December, 1956.

8. Katz, M. "Improving Classroom Tests by Means of Item Analysis." *The Clearing House*. January, 1961, 265-269.

9. Odell, C. W. *How To Improve Classroom Testing*. Dubuque, Iowa: William C. Brown, 1953.

10. Thomas, R. M. *Judging Student Progress*. New York: Longmans, Green and Co., 1954. Chapter 3.

11. Thorndike, R. L. and Hagen, Elizabeth. *Measurement and Evaluation in Psychology and Education*. New York: John C. Wiley and Sons, 1955. Chapters 3 and 4.

12. Wood, Dorothy A. *Test Construction*. Columbus: Merrill, 1960.

9. Checklist for Reviewing Local School Tests

Sherman N. Tinkelman

    This checklist covers the major test construction principles which teachers should observe in the preparation of local school tests. A negative answer to any question in the checklist indicates variation of local practice from accepted principles of test construction, suggesting that a reevaluation of local practice may be desirable with a view toward possible improvement of the test.

    The items in the checklist cannot be added like the items of an examination to provide a "score" for a local school test. The questions are not of equal importance. Though a test may be satisfactory in all respects but one, that single deficiency may be sufficient to impair seriously the value of the test as a whole. The purpose of the checklist, rather, is diagnostic. It is designed to help insure that in the development of a local school test no important factor likely to influence the effectiveness of the test will be overlooked.

The Test Items

A. Essay Questions

    1. Are essay questions restricted to measurement of objectives not readily measured by other item types?

    2. Are essay questions framed around specific problems, adequately delimited in scope?

From *Improving the Classroom Test*, Albany, New York: Bureau of Examinations and Testing, University of the State of New York, 1957. Reprinted by permission from Sherman N. Tinkelman.

    3. In general, is use made of a large number of brief essays rather than one or two extended essays?

    4. Does each essay question indicate clearly and accurately the desired extent and depth of the answer?

       a. Does the question indicate clearly how many reasons, examples, arguments, etc. are expected for full credit?

       b. Do the directions to "explain," "outline," "state," "compare" etc. indicate accurately the type of answer that will receive full credit?

B. Completion Items

    1. Is each statement sufficiently unambiguous to limit the correct answer to one or two specific words or phrases?

    2. Is an excessive number of blank spaces avoided?

    3. Does the omitted part of each question come at the end or near the end of the statement?

    4. Are the items free from extraneous clues due to grammatical structure, length of blank space, etc.?

    5. Is use of the completion form generally avoided when items are essentially true-false in nature?

    6. Do computational problems indicate the expected degree of precision in the answer?

       a. Does the question indicate clearly the extent to which approximations or fractional answers are to be rounded?

       b. Does the question indicate clearly whether units (such as square yards or feet per second) are to be included by the pupil in his answer?

C. True-False Items

    1. Is each item definite and unambiguous in meaning?

    2. Are the items based upon statements that are absolutely true or false, without qualifications or exceptions?

    3. Has the central point of each question been highlighted by placing it in a prominent position?

4. Are the items free from double-barreled statements that are partly true and partly false?
5. Are the items expressed as simply and directly as possible, without many qualifying clauses?
6. Are trick questions avoided?
7. Is excessive "window dressing" in the items avoided?
8. Are negative questions avoided so far as possible?
9. Are the items free from specific determiners such as "always" and "usually"?
10. In the modified true-false type of item, is the word to be corrected clearly indicated by underlining or special type?

D. Multiple-Choice Items

1. Is use of the direct question or incomplete statement form consistent with the most effective presentation of the individual items?
2. Are the items presented in clear and simple language, with vocabulary kept as simple as possible?
3. Does each item have one and only one correct answer?
4. Is each item concerned with a single central problem?
5. Is the central problem of each item stated clearly and completely in the stem?
6. Does the stem, so far as possible, include all words repeated in the responses?
7. Are negative statements avoided?
8. Is excessive "window dressing" avoided?
9. Do the responses or choices come at the ends of the incomplete statements?
10. Are the responses grammatically consistent with the stem and parallel with one another in form?
11. Are all responses plausible and attractive to pupils who lack the information or ability tested by the item?
12. Are the responses, so far as possible, arranged in numerical or logical order?
13. Are the responses independent and mutually exclusive?

14. Are the items free from extraneous clues due to grammatical inconsistencies, rote verbal associations, length of response, etc.?
15. Is the "none-of-these" option used only when appropriate?

E. Matching Items

1. Do the premises and responses constitute homogeneous lists, each grouped around a single concept?
2. Are the lists of premises and responses relatively short?
3. Are the matching lists conveniently arranged?
   a. Are the longer, more complex statements used as premises and the shorter statements as responses?
   b. Wherever possible, are the responses arranged in some logical order to simplify matching?
4. Do the directions indicate clearly the basis upon which the lists are to be matched?
   a. If a single premise is to be matched with several responses, is the pupil advised that this is permissible?
   b. If a single response is to be matched with several premises, is the pupil advised that this is permissible?
5. Are the matching lists free from extraneous clues due to grammatical construction, rote verbal associations, etc.?
6. Is the list of responses longer than the list of premises to preclude guessing by elimination?

Mechanical Features of the Test

A. Item Format

1. Are the items in the test numbered?
2. Is each item complete on a page?
3. Does the reference material for an item appear on the same page as the item or on a facing page?
4. Are the item responses arranged to achieve both legibility and economy of space?

B. Scoring Arrangements
1. Has consideration been given to the practicability of a separate answer sheet?
2. Are answers to be indicated by symbols rather than underlining or copying?
3. Are answer spaces placed in a vertical column for easy scoring?
4. If answer spaces are placed at the right of the page, is each answer space clearly associated with its corresponding item?
5. Are the answer symbols to be used by the pupils free from possible ambiguity due to careless penmanship or deliberate hedging?
6. Are the answer symbols to be used by the pupils free from confusion with the substance or content of the responses?

C. Distribution of Correct Responses
1. Are correct answers distributed so that the same answer does not appear in a long series of consecutive questions?
2. Are correct answers distributed to avoid an excessive proportion of items in the test with the same answer?
3. Is patterning of answers in a fixed repeating sequence avoided?

D. Grouping and Arrangement of Items
1. Are items of the same type requiring the same directions grouped together in the test?
2. Where juxtaposition of items of markedly dissimilar content is likely to cause confusion, are items grouped by content within each item type grouping?
3. Are items generally arranged from easy to more difficult within the test as a whole and within each major subdivision of the test?

E. Designating Credit Allowances
1. Are credits indicated for the major sections of the test?
2. Is the credit allowance for each item clear to the pupil?

3. Where questions have subdivisions, especially in essay questions, are credits indicated for each of the parts of the question?

F. Directions for Answering Questions
   1. Are simple, clear and specific directions given for each different item type in the test?
   2. Are directions clearly set off from the rest of the test by appropriate spacing or type style?
   3. Is effective use made of sample questions and answers to help clarify directions for unusual item types?

G. Correction for Guessing
   1. If deductions are to be made for wrong answers, are pupils instructed not to guess?
   2. If no deductions are to be made for wrong answers, are pupils advised to answer every question according to their best judgment?

H. Allowing Choice of Items
   1. Is the degree of choice sufficiently limited, and are the questions among which choice is allowed sufficiently similar in difficulty, to maintain reasonable comparability of pupils' scores?
   2. Are the directions covering choice prominent, clear and explicit?
   3. Is choice exercised within relatively small groups of items rather than among many items?

I. Printing and Duplicating
   1. Has the test been duplicated to provide individual pupil copies?
   2. Is the test free from annoying and confusing typographical errors?
   3. Is the legibility of the test satisfactory from the viewpoint of type size, adequacy of spacing and clarity of printing?
   4. Is the length of line neither too long nor too short for easy comprehension?

10. Short-Cut Statistics for Teacher-Made Tests

Paul B. Diederich

For the Non-mathematical Teacher

The writer is an ex-Latin-teacher with thirty years of teaching experience who was attracted to testing by the fact that so much nonsense is written and spoken about education. He wanted to find out, at least in his own classes, what worked and what did not work by means of tests of his own construction—both essay tests and objective tests. Since it took him longer than he cared to spend to analyze his test results by the precise and elegant methods favored by statisticians, he gradually learned or developed short cuts that yielded approximately the same results.

All of these short cuts have passed two basic tests. First, they were all applied to actual data by the writer's son while he was in the eighth grade, making B's in arithmetic, and he had no trouble with the mathematics. Second, they have all been discussed with competent statisticians who winced slightly but agreed that the methods are valid for the purposes for which most teachers will use them, and as precise as the data from classroom tests will ordinarily warrant.

Item-analysis

Item-analysis by a show of hands.

One of the chief advantages of published tests over teacher-made tests is that the former are pretested on a large number of students like those for whom the test is intended, and then the professional test-maker gets figures on (a) the success of the group on each item (what percent got it right); (b) the discriminating power of each item (based on how many more high-scoring than low-scoring students got it right); and (c) how many high-scoring and low-scoring students chose each response to each item. The test-maker then discards items that are too hard, too easy, or non-discriminating, or else touches up items by revising some responses or substituting others. Usually at least half of the items that are pretested in this way are either discarded or revised, and the final form of the test contains only items that are likely to work well.

Teachers cannot pretest items for important tests on the same group that is to take the final forms of these tests, for that would show them what questions were going to be asked, and students would bone up on them. However, if teachers item-analyze each important test *after* it is given, they can gradually build up a file of test items that have worked well in the past or have been revised to eliminate faults that appeared in earlier forms. This file will both reduce the work of constructing tests and improve the tests. If the file is large (as it very soon will be), students seldom learn what questions to expect. Examiners report very little tendency for old items to get "easier" as the years roll on.

Unfortunately, the only way of making an item-analysis that is explained in the books on tests and measurements is so laborious and time-consuming that no teacher who has tried it once is ever likely to try it again. It consists of preparing a form and then putting down a tally for each student's response to every question—in other words, copying all answers to all questions. If there are 40 questions in the test and 40 students, that means putting down 1,600 tallies. If one is careful, it also means checking every tally, since nothing is easier to misplace than a tally. If one skips an item, for example, all of the tallies down to the point at which one discovers the error will record the student's answers to the wrong questions. Hence there will be at least 3,200 operations to perform, not counting the correction of errors, for each forty-minute test in one class. It is not surprising, therefore, that item-analysis is almost never applied to teacher-made tests, even though it is the basic operation that all published tests have to undergo and the basic reason for whatever superiority they possess.

Yet all of this work can be done by a show of hands in class in so little time that students do not resent it. It adds greatly to their understanding of the test and is a better basis for class discussion of items that gave trouble than having students suggest items to discuss. The bright students are naturally the first to respond, and they tend to suggest items that present subtle problems of interpretation. One may never get to the items that reveal the basic weaknesses of the class.

For routine tests, the teacher may call out the numbers of the items one by one. Each student holding a paper that got that item *wrong* holds up his hand. The teacher counts and announces the number of hands that he sees for each item, and writes that number opposite the item on his own copy of the test, encircling items that call for discussion. It goes like this:

"Item 1. How many of you are holding a paper that got item 1 wrong? Hold up your hands. I see three hands. Anyone else? Let me repeat my question to make sure that you have this straight. Look at item 1. Is it marked right or wrong? If it is marked *wrong,* hold up your hands. I now see four hands. Larry, what was the trouble? You thought I meant *right?* No, that is the other kind of item-analysis; here I just want to find out which items gave us the most trouble. Now go on to item 2. Hands? I see two hands. Item 3? No hands. Did nobody get it wrong? Very good. Item 4. I see fourteen hands; we'll have to discuss that one. Item 5, zero. Item 6, two."

And so on. Remember that the teacher records the number of errors opposite each item on his own copy of the test, and encircles questions that enough students missed to warrant discussion.

For more important tests, the teacher may want the "high-low" type of item-analysis that will also reveal the discriminating power of each item, as shown by the fact that more high-scoring than low-scoring students got it right. Professionals use the top 27% in total scores on the test as the "high" group, the bottom 27% as the "low." If the teacher uses these proportions, he can use the *Item Analysis Table* prepared by Chung-Teh Fan in 1952 (available through Evaluation and Advisory Service, Educational Testing Service, at two dollars per copy) to look up all the item-statistics discussed in the following section.

The writer, who has been conducting these item-counts by a show of hands for years in his own classes, prefers using top and bottom *halves* for the reason that otherwise the whole middle half of the class has nothing to do during the item-analysis and feels left out and gets into mischief. One must expect smaller differences in per cent correct than one would get between the top and bottom 27%, but it is still quite clear how much of a difference is desirable. It ought to be at least 10% of the class. In a class of 40 students, at least four more students in the top half than in the bottom half should get an item right.

This figure was not chosen at random or by rule-of-thumb. Here we must get just a bit technical for a moment, because part of the fun is the pure swank of knowing what the experts are talking about, and knowing that one has comparable figures for one's own tests. The index of discrimination that they use is called the "biserial correlation with total test." It is a decimal that shows to what extent success on the item is related to success on the test as a whole. Putting it another way, it tells the extent to which people who did well on the whole test did better on this particular item than people who did poorly on the whole test. The professionals like to have their *average* biserial above .4 and are quite proud of themselves if it hits .5 or above. They look hard at items with biserials below .3 and either touch them up or get rid of them unless they can prove on other grounds that the item is a good item that is not closely related to the rest of the test.

Now, it just happens that, for items in the middle range of difficulty (that 25% to 75% of the students answered correctly), the biserial correlation with total test is approximately equal to three times the high-low difference, expressed as a per cent of the class. This is true when the high-low difference is based on high-low *halves* of the class—not otherwise. If the high-low difference is four, and this is 10% of the class (of 40 students), the biserial correlation of this item with the total test will be approximately .30. If it is six, or 15% of the class, the biserial will be approximately .45. This approximation does not get seriously wrong until one reaches items that more than 80% or fewer than 20% of the class answered correctly. For these extremely easy or extremely difficult items, it is usually a serious *under*estimate of the true biserial. One consolation is that, while such items may be highly discriminating, they discriminate for a very small fraction of the group. Still, one occasionally wants a very easy or a very hard item. In such cases a high-low difference of even 5% of the class may be quite acceptable, and certainly anything higher is hard to get, but the difference between high-low halves is not a good index at these extremes.

Do not fear that you will have to compute these per cents for every item. When you begin each item-analysis, divide the number of students who are present by 10 and round to the nearest whole number. If 38 are present, the minimum acceptable high-low difference will be 4. If an item exceeds this number, its discrimination is satisfactory; if not, you will have to look at it to see whether anything is wrong.

After you or the students have finished scoring the test, arrange the papers in descending order of total scores and count down to the middle score. Suppose this score is 21, and five students made it. All papers above this score obviously go into the high group; those below go into the low. But what about the five middle papers? Put them at random into the high and low piles until the numbers in each pile are equal. If you have an odd number of students, hold out one middle paper and do not count it in the item-analysis. The student who does not get a paper will be the score-keeper and will write the figures for each item on the blackboard; otherwise the teacher will do it.

Now it is necessary to have a clear separation between the "highs" and the "lows" in the classroom. To avoid shifting the students, those on the right may get the high papers, those on the left the low; or those in front may get the highs, those in back the lows. The teacher appoints a counter for each group to call out the number of hands raised in his part of the room for each item.

The four figures obtained for each item may be labeled and defined as follows:

H = the number of highs who got the item right
L = the number of lows who get the item right
$H + L$ = "SUCCESS" (the *total* number who get the item right)
$H - L$ = "DISCRIMINATION" or "the high-low *difference*" (how many more highs than lows got the item right)

The teacher calls out the numbers of the items one by one: e.g., "Item 1." Everyone whose paper got that item right holds up his hand. The counter for the highs calls out the number of upraised hands in his section: e.g., "Fourteen." Then the counter for the lows calls out the number of upraised hands in his section: e.g., "Eight." The scorekeeper, be he teacher or student, immediately adds these two figures and calls out the *total*: e.g., "Twenty-two." He than subtracts the lows from the highs (in his head) and calls out the *difference*: e.g., "Six." Everyone copies these four figures at the bottom of item 1 on the copy of the test that he is holding: 14. 8. 22. 6. There is no need to label them, since this is a standard sequence, and before long everyone will know what it means. The rhythm of the operation is approximately as follows: Item 1. Hands. Pause for counting. 14. 8. 22. 6. Item 2. . . . If the teacher or a student wants to call for any of these figures again, the proper short form of the question is, "What was the high? the low? the total? the difference?"

After a little practice, the complete item-analysis for a one-period test will take between ten and twenty minutes, depending on the number of items. It would take the teacher at least two hours to do it at home, and he would make far more mistakes than will be made in class, where every alert student will be only too happy to pounce on any mistake in counting, adding, or subtracting. Teachers in the writer's measurement classes have conducted such item-analyses as far down as the fourth grade and have reported that the students had no trouble understanding the procedure or carrying it out. At the other end of the scale, even students in graduate courses do not resent it. It gives them visual, auditory, and tactile clues to the success of the class on each item, and it shows them graphically and convincingly which items separated the sheep from the goats. They get personally involved in finding out how well the class did on the test, and why they went wrong on the items that gave trouble. By contrast, if the teacher does all the work for them at home and hands them the results of his analysis on a platter, no one will understand and no one will be interested. They have to get into the act if the analysis of a test is to be a moving and enlightening experience.

Standards for Test Items: Success.

It is a common belief that most tests should start with very easy items, gradually get harder, and end with very hard items. If this sequence is hard to arrange, at least the test should cover a very wide range of item-difficulties. While many professionals share this view, it is worth knowing that practically every serious investigation of this problem since 1932 has come up with the opposite conclusion: that precision of measurement is greatest when all of the items in a test are about equally difficult for the group tested; that maximum reliability and dispersion of scores will be attained if every item in the usual sort of multiple-choice test is answered correctly by somewhere between 60% and 70% of the students tested. We do not want to insist on this point, since the advantage of a narrow range of item-difficulties is very small in relation to other sources of validity and reliability, and since it is usually almost impossible to achieve a narrow range of item-difficulties. Still, teachers should know that if they sweat hard in order to achieve a nice progression from easy to difficult, their effort has probably been wasted, and its most probable effect will be precisely the contrary of what they expect. They expect it to yield a wider spread of scores. What it actually yields is a narrower spread of scores than if all the items were of approximately equal difficulty. Hence items that more than 90% got right should be questioned as too easy, and items that fewer than 30% got right as too hard for inclusion in a test. Questioned, mind you, not rejected—for they may be justified on other grounds.

Standards for Test Items: Discrimination

It has already been indicated that the minimum acceptable high-low difference by professional standards is 10% of the class, and why this is so, except in very easy and very hard items. The "standard error" of this sort of high-low difference, however, is so large that at least a fifth of the items that turn out to be quite discriminating after repeated use may fall below this standard in any one administration of the test by pure chance. Hence we should be wary of rejecting an item if it falls below the suggested minimum the first time it is tried if, after due consideration, we can find nothing wrong with the item. It is quite strict enough to say that not more than a fifth of the items in the final test should fall below this standard, and the *average* high-low difference should be above 10% of the class—preferably 15% or above. High discrimination spreads out the scores as widely as possible and hence increases the reliability of the test.

A teacher who uses this method of item-analysis will soon find out that high-low differences for some of his items will be zero or negative: that is, the same number of students in the top and bottom halves may get them right, or more low-scoring than high-scoring students may pick the keyed answer. One of the chief uses of item-analysis is to direct attention to such items. While this sort of thing can happen by pure chance, a closer look at the item will often reveal why the better students shied away from the intended answer. One can touch up the ambiguity or inaccuracy and thereby save not only the item but the resentment of future students who would be bright enough to detect the error.

All discrimination figures look wonderful toward the end of a test that only the high-scoring students were able to finish. For example, it may appear that almost all of the high-scoring students and none of the low-scoring students answered the last item correctly— which would be ideal if it were not spurious. All the low-scoring students might have known the answer but simply did not reach the item. After a fifth of the students have dropped out, item-analysis figures are so misleading that it is well not to continue the analysis beyond this point.

Second Stage of Item-Analysis

There may be a few items in a test that turned out to be too easy, too hard, or did not discriminate satisfac- torily for no apparent reason, and class discussion does not reveal anything wrong with them. If there is time, these may be subjected to a second stage of item- analysis, which is too laborious and time-consuming to apply to more than a few items. For these few items, one asks how many in the high group, and then how many in the low group (a) omitted the item, and (b) chose each response. Results like the following may indicate what is wrong:

	Omit	Responses				
		1	2	3	4	5
High	0	11	9	0	0	0
Low	0	14	4	2	0	0

The right answer, response 1, is indicated by a line between the highs and lows who chose it. Three more lows than highs chose it; hence its index of discrimina- tion is −3. Why? The figures for response 2 suggest an answer. This response was too attractive to the high- scoring students. Perhaps they thought response 1 was too obvious; they suspected a trap; then they figured out some interpretation of response 2 that they could defend as the right answer. If so, discussion should reveal what interpretation they gave to response 2, and it can be revised in a way that does not permit this interpretation. At the same time, responses 4 and 5 might be made a shade more plausible, but still definitely wrong, because in their present form they were wasted; nobody chose them. Incidentally, item-analysis has probably been a factor in reducing the five-choice item, which was standard a generation ago, to the four-choice item which is more popular today except in a few item-types (such as spelling) in which the fifth response is usually "none of these." Item-writers were not very successful in framing five responses that were all sufficiently plausible to "draw blood."

The Standard Error

The Standard Error of a Test Score

Since we have already introduced the concept of "standard error" in connection with high-low differences, this may be a good time to extend the concept to test scores. The first thing to be said about it is that the standard error is not computed in the same way in these two cases and is not of anything like the same magnitude. If you look in the index of a textbook of elementary statistics, you will find at least fifteen different kinds of standard errors: of scores, averages, differences, correlations, proportions, etc. They are all computed differently and yield figures of different orders of magnitude. The standard error of an average, for example, is usually much smaller than the standard error of a single score, while the standard error of the difference between two scores is larger than the standard error of either score. They all have this basic meaning in common, however. Suppose you repeated a certain measurement operation a hundred times and kept averaging the results until no further repetitions would change that average one iota. You may think of that final average as the "true" measure, no matter whether it is a score on spelling, the average of a class, the difference between two classes, the correlation between spelling and verbal intelligence, or whatnot. You might then mark off the points that would enclose the middle two-thirds of the figures you got on the various trials on your way to that final average. You would call these points one standard error above the true measure and one standard error below it. You might then go on to mark the points that would enclose the middle 95% of all the figures you got on the various trials. You would call these points two standard errors above the true measure and two standard errors below. There would still be 5% of extremely deviant figures beyond these two points, but the limits of two standard errors would enclose most of the figures that you would get.

The trouble with applying this concept to testing is that we are never sure what the "true" measure is, since we do not have time in schools to measure the same attribute a hundred times, and if we did, we would change it beyond recognition. But statistical theory permits us to compute the standard error of most measurement operations on the first trial, and then we can say that the chances are two out of three that the obtained figure lies within one standard error of the true figure, and 95 out of 100 that it lies within two standard errors.

The next thing to be said about the standard error is that it is not the same as the "probable error" that was popular a generation ago, but it is based on the same idea of the limits within which measures may vary by pure chance, and either figure may be translated into the other. The chief reason why the "probable error" is no longer used is that there is no way to compute it directly; one first has to compute the standard error and then take approximately two-thirds of it to get the probable error. The only point in doing so was that the early statisticians thought it would be easier for the hayseeds to grasp the idea that the chances were fifty-fifty that the obtained figure would lie within one "probable error" of the true figure, rather than that the chances were two to one that it would lie within one "standard error." On mature reflection, however, it seemed that the first idea was not really any easier to grasp than the second, and it was rather silly to keep on performing an extra operation every time one computed an error of measurement just to make the figure more appealing to the laity. The name "probable error" undeniably had more popular appeal, but the appeal was spurious on two counts. First, this kind of "error" is not "probable"; it is certain. Second, it gave the idea that someone may have made that much of a mistake in taking the measure. If any such mistakes are made, they are not included within this type of "error." It must be understood in its root sense of "variation." It assumes that all the measures have been taken and recorded accurately; even so, you are not going to get the same figure twice except by luck. The "error" indicates within what limits the obtained figures are likely to vary by pure chance.

Not all kinds of chance, however. If a teacher gets angry at the students who were absent during a crucial examination and sees to it that the make-up test is harder and marked more severely, their scores will dip in a way that could not be predicted mathematically. *Mistakes* in writing items, scoring, or marking unintended answers and *external circumstances* that may affect scores, such as sickness, noise, interruptions, hot sticky days, etc., are also beyond the pale of the standard error. The only kind of variation in scores that is standard and therefore measurable is "sampling error." Suppose you want to find out how well your students can spell. There are at least 600,000 English words that you might ask them to spell, but let us suppose that there are only 10,000 that they would ordinarily be asked to spell by the end of grade 6. If you select 100 of these words completely at random and get an accurate score on the number they were able to spell, the score will give you an estimate of the percentage of the 10,000 words that they are probably able to spell. But it you take another 100 words from the same pool of words completely at random, you know that very few students will get exactly the same score as on the first 100. This variation, due to the sample that happens to be chosen, is what the standard error means.

The variation will be much larger if two different teachers independently try to find out how well the same class appreciates *Hamlet*. Here the number of valid questions that they might ask is theoretically infinite, but each has time to ask only 40 questions. If we can regard each set of questions as a random sample drawn from an infinite pool of items testing the same ability, the variation in scores from one such sample to another is the sort of thing that is measured by the standard error. In practice, the variation will be much greater, since the teacher's bias will affect his selection of questions: one may be a bear on character development, the other on figures of speech. They are not measuring the same attribute at all, even though both call it "appreciation of *Hamlet*."

For these reasons, the standard error accounts for only a small part of the variation in scores that may be expected in practice, but it is quite large enough to make us want to get several independent scores before we make up our minds as to the degree of success of our students in attaining the objectives of the course. The standard error tells within what limits scores may be expected to vary by pure chance *in the selection of items.* If we add to that our own *bias* in the selection of items, the *stupid mistakes* we make in writing the items and in scoring them, and *external circumstances* that may affect the ability of the student to answer the questions, it is obvious that the variation we may expect between two independent measures of an ability that we refer to by a single name may be quite large. It is not so large, however, that we should despair of ever being able to find out which of our students have been more successful than others in attaining the objectives of the course. Since we usually have them for a full year, we need never rely on a single measure but can give them a long series of measures. Any one measure is like any one baseball game, in which the team that is in the cellar may clobber the team at the top. But over the whole season, the team that is really superior will rise to the top, and the team that is really inferior will fall to the bottom.

This table may be interpreted as follows: In an objective test of 50 items, two scores out of three will lie within 4 raw-score points (one standard error) of the "true score" these students would attain if you continued testing with repeated random samples from the universe of items testing the same ability, and 95% of the scores will lie within 8 raw-score points (two standard errors) of "true scores." The relatively few scores at the extremes will have slightly smaller standard errors, as indicated under "Exceptions," but there are usually not enough of these to justify separate treatment.

Estimated Standard Errors of Test Scores:

Number of Items	Standard Error	Exceptions: Regardless of the Length of Test, the Standard Error is:
$<$ 24	2	0 when the score is zero or perfect;
24–47	3	1 when 1 or 2 points from 0 or from 100%;
48–89	4	2 when 3 to 7 points from 0 or from 100%;
90–109	5	3 when 8 to 15 points from 0 or from 100%.
110–129	6	
130–150	7	

If your local Director of Research casts aspersions on this table, ask him to read two articles by Frederic M. Lord, "Do Tests of the Same Length Have the Same Standard Errors of Measurement?" and "Tests of the Same Length Do Have the Same Standard Error of Measurement" in *Educational and Psychological Measurement,* XVII, 4 (Winter, 1957): 510-521; and XIX, 2 (Summer, 1959): 233-239.

When Are Two Test Scores "Really" Different?

The Cooperative Test Division of Educational Testing Service has been the first major test publisher to enforce attention to the standard error of test scores by reporting scores on its new SCAT and STEP tests as bands rather than as points. Each "band" extends from one standard error below the obtained score to one standard error above, and it is explained that the chances are two out of three that the "true" score lies somewhere within this band. Teachers are urged not to regard two scores as "really" different unless the two bands do not overlap: i.e., unless the two scores are at least two standard errors apart.

While this is a great improvement over previous practice in interpreting differences between scores, a teacher who has managed to read this far without losing his grip may want to carry this line of thinking a step further in order to get hold of the concept of "the standard error of a difference." It was indicated in passing on page 9 that the standard error of a difference between two scores is larger than the standard error of either score. Think of the difference as a rope tied between two stakes, which are the two scores. Since there is wobble in both stakes, there is bound to be more wobble in the rope than there is in either stake.

To get the standard error of the difference between two scores, square the standard error of each score, add the two squares, and take the square root. For example, it was shown on page 12 that the standard error of a test of 24–47 items is 3 (rounded to the nearest whole number). Three squared is nine, the square of the standard error of each score. Nine plus nine is eighteen, the sum of the squares of the standard errors of two such scores. The square root of 18 is approximately 4¼. This is the standard error of the *difference* between the two scores. You can see at once that it is appreciably larger than the standard error of either score, which is 3.

Now, if you want to be 95% sure that the two scores represent a true difference in ability, the difference between them ought to be twice the standard error of the *difference*—not twice the standard error of either score. In other words, the two scores should be at least 8½ points apart, not just 6 points apart as the Cooperative Test recommendation implies. The Cooperative people are well aware of this point but do not use it in reporting scores because (1) it would be too complicated for teachers to square, add, and take a square root before comparing any two scores; (2) if two bands do not overlap, they usually do not touch, and the distance between them is likely to reach statistical "significance"; (3) even when they do touch, the difference between the two scores is "significant" at about the 15% level, which is good enough for most classroom purposes.

Levels of Significance.

When people report "findings" rather than "opinions," it is common practice for them to tag each "finding" as

**(significant at the 1% level);
 *(significant at the 5% level);
NS(not significant).

The last is professional shorthand for "not significant even at the 5% level." Thus, the difference between two Cooperative Test scores whose bands touched but did not overlap would be reported as "not significant"—significant only at the 15% level. That is, out of every 100 differences of exactly this size, 15 might be due to pure chance in the selection of items for the test. In any one of these cases, there is no way to tell whether the difference was "real." One can only report, after computing the "wobble" in the measure, that there are 15 chances in a hundred that it might have been a fluke. That is commonly regarded as "not significant."

It is obvious from this that a statistician is a man who, if he remains true to his principles, would never bet on horse-races. He is willing to say that a difference is "real" (i.e., not a chance difference) only if there are less than five chances in a hundred that the obtained difference could have come about by accident of sampling. Even this is considered rather a grave risk, and he is really happy only when there is less than one chance in a hundred that the difference was a fluke. Since he also has a knack for inventing names that mean the opposite of what the layman would think he meant, he calls these two points "the 5% level" and "the 1% level." These sound as though the second was less significant than the first, but the opposite is true. The first means that there are less than five chances in a hundred that the difference is a fluke; the second that there is less than one chance in a hundred. Although he would shudder at the loose language, surely we are justified as laymen in thinking of the first as "95% sure" and the second as "99% sure" that the difference is "real". We ought, however, to be sure-footed in our definitions of these looser terms. "Real," for example, here means only "non-chance." It does not necessarily mean "true," for if an experiment was set up by a very biased person, it might yield results that were the opposite of the truth (as it ultimately emerges from the consensus of later investigators). It would still be proper to say that the results obtained by the first investigator did not arise by chance—by accident of sampling. They arose from bias.

Since bias, stupidity, and carelessness seem far more likely to the layman to vitiate the results of experiments than pure chance, he wonders whether it is worth while to discount the effect of chance alone. The answer seems to be that it *is* worth while, chiefly because almost all educational measurements contain so large an element of pure chance that many score differences can be attributed to accidents of sampling. The critic can go on to consider whether the remaining differences are true and important, or simply the logical result of the stupid and biased way in which the experiment was conducted.

But how does one establish these two levels of "significance"? First, a difference is significant at the 5% level if the difference is twice as large as its own standard error (not the standard error of the two scores, but the standard error of the difference). It is significant at the 1% level if the difference is 2.6 times as large as its own standard error. You divide the difference by its own standard error, and if the quotient is between 2 and 2.6, you are in the clear; if it is 2.6 or more, you are on velvet—or, as the statistician would say, "not in the chance domain." There is, of course, no reason to set any particular limit as the boundary between reality and chance, but the 5% and 1% levels of significance are most commonly reported for the sake of simplicity. There are many other "tests of significance," but this one is probably the most widely used in educational research, and sufficiently representative to give you the basic idea.

Philosophic Digression

Since it is as hard for the writer as for an equally non-mathematical reader to keep his mind on the mathematics of the testing situation, perhaps we both may be forgiven for pausing a moment to cackle over the rather odd definition of reality that has come to be accepted as a rule of the game by people who are searching for reality in the supremely important area of the growth of the mind. Such people may be visualized as primitive parents who are standing the minds of their children up against the back door and measuring the aspects of those minds that they know how to measure at all with a foot-rule that stretches or contracts every time it is used. All that they feel safe in saying about their measures is that two-thirds of the time they come within an inch of the true figure, but five per cent of the time they are more than two inches off. Therefore, before they say that the mind of Susie has grown up more than the mind of Joe toward such a goal as the appreciation of *Hamlet,* they ask that the difference between them be at least twice the amount that the ruler will stretch (or contract) in measuring such differences, and preferably 2.6 times that amount. Since the standard error of any one measurement with this ruler is one inch, its standard error in measuring a difference will be—how much?

Square the standard error of Susie's measurement. $1^2 = 1.$
Square the standard error of Joe's measurement. $1^2 = \underline{1.}$
Add the two squares.   2
Take the square root.   1.4

Thus the standard error of our ruler in measuring a *difference* is 1.4 inches. (If you do not know how to extract square roots, any math teacher can give you a table of squares and square roots of numbers between 1 and 1,000.) Then, by the rules of the Ancient and Honorable Order of Measurers, we are allowed to certify that Susie is bigger than Joe in appreciating *Hamlet* only if she is at least 2.8 inches bigger on our fallible foot-rule (twice the standard error of our instrument in measuring differences). If other members of the tribe want to know how certain that verdict is, we can tell them that, if there were no true difference, an apparent difference as large as this would turn up less than five times in a hundred measurements of the same kind. If they have an immense prize of a ton of gold for the best appreciator of *Hamlet* (surely a wise investment for any community) and want to be surer than that, we can insist that Susie be at least 3.6 inches bigger on this wobbly instrument (2.6 times the standard error of the instrument in measuring differences). Then we can certify that the chances are less than one in a hundred that we would get a difference as large as this if there were no true difference.

Obviously there will be a great clamor among the more ignorant members of the tribe that this is no way to go about it; the thing to do is to buy a steel foot-rule that will not stretch or squeeze on every measurement and that will yield absolutely exact results. Alas, there are no such instruments for measuring the growth of the mind, and we have to put up with those we have. Of course, there will be members of the tribe who will insist that they can ask Susie and Joe five questions about *Hamlet* and tell you for sure which one appreciates it best, but such people will be found to differ far more widely in their verdicts than will the measurers.

"All exact science," says Bertrand Russell in *The Scientific Outlook,* "is dominated by the idea of *approximation*. When a man tells you that he knows the exact truth about anything, you are safe in inferring that he is an *inexact* man."

Most of philosophy, as well, has been concerned in one way or another with the problem of distinguishing *appearance* from *reality*. Like the poor educator who gets fed up with the vast amount of nonsense that is talked and written about education, and who turns to testing to find something that is *real* as a basis for his deductions, the philosophers have been busy since the beginning of time with the problem of separating truth from opinion—warranted assertibility from mere assertion. While they have done a great deal to clarify the problem, there are not too many instances in which they have come up with widely understood and accepted rules to guide the seeker of reality. Among these are the rules of logic and the canons of scientific investigation. Far down among the latter is the convention that a difference may be accepted as real (as caused by something other than the vagaries of the measuring instrument) only if it is twice as great as the standard error of the instrument in measuring differences, and preferably 2.6 times as great. That sort of ground-rule for conducting an inquiry into the truth about education would have interested Plato, and he would probably have approved of it, since he was a good mathematician himself and regarded mathematics as a basic discipline for anyone seriously interested in the search for reality.

A few disgraceful members of the teaching profession may wonder why anyone should have any trouble discovering what is real about education. What is real about it, they will tell you, is the sweat, the smell, the noise, the trouble with discipline, the overcrowded classes, the low pay, and so on. If anyone professes to find reality in education by the process of computing standard errors of differences, they will hoot with derision. We might agree that these are some of the unpleasant realities in the *job* of educating as it is now conducted, but we are not interested in them; we want to find out what is real in the *process* of educating: that is, in assisting the growth of the mind (not just in general but in specified dimensions, such as in spelling, in arithmetic, in reading comprehension, and so on up to the appreciation of *Hamlet*). If we looked for such growth amid the noise and smells of the classroom of the naive realist, we might find none at all. Who, then, is overlooking the reality: the measurer who does not care about the noise, or the realist who does not care about education? Both ignore certain aspects of reality, but the part that the realist excludes from consideration seems to many level-headed people far more important.

At another end of the spectrum are some very nice people who find what is real in education in the light that is in the eyes of the children, in the lilt of their voices, in the cute things they say, and in the charm of their artistic productions. They, also, would deplore the quest for a reality that is certified by two standard errors. But they would also have to assent to the proposition that their job is not limited to keeping students happy and creative; they have to assist the growth of the mind; and it is their hypothesis that happiness and creativity assist that growth better than blood, sweat, and tears. Very well—but that hypothesis requires evidence. The evidence cannot be that the children are in fact happy and creative. It must show that they learn more than when they are unhappy and uncreative. And to show that they learn *more*—there you have a difference, and it is good discipline in thinking about education to refuse to recognize it as "real" unless it is at least twice as great as the standard error in measuring such differences.

The Standard Error of An Average

While the reader may look upon this heading gloomily as "more of the same," the proper response to it, if he only knew, is "Hope begins to dawn," or "The United States Marines are coming!"

He must have wondered how he could ever prove that any distance between two points in education was real, when the foot-rule we conjured up for measuring appreciation of *Hamlet* was, in common language, "accurate within one inch," yet the minimum difference we could certify as real turned out to be 2.8 inches. Also, the standard error of most classroom tests is about three raw-score points, yet the minimum difference between two scores that we could certify as real (at the 5% level) was 8½ points. At that rate, all that we could assert about the distribution of scores on most classroom tests would be that most of the students in the top quarter of scores on this test were probably superior to most students in the bottom quarter. We could make no assertion with confidence about the scores of the middle half of the class.

All of this is sad but true; there is very little hope of proving anything in education with single measures. The real hope lies in repeated measurements; either testing many students with each single measure, or testing the same student with many different measures in the course of the year. The reason is that the standard error of an *average* is much smaller than the standard errors of the scores that enter into it. With each additional case or measure, the standard error gets smaller, until in practice it is really not difficult to prove that some things work better than others, or that some students are superior to others with respect to any given objective.

The way to compute the standard error of a class average is to divide the "standard deviation" of the scores by the square root of the number of students. If you are averaging many tests of the same ability (on the same score-scale) for a single student, you divide the "standard deviation" of his scores by the square root of the number of tests. The more general statement that takes in both of these cases is that *the standard error of an average is the standard deviation of the measures divided by the square root of the number of measures.* If the number of measures is less than thirty, you are supposed to divide by the square root of one less than the number of measures ($\sqrt{N-1}$).

Now we have to find out what the "standard deviation" is and how to compute it. This is more important than you may think, for practically every other statistic that you will ever compute has the "standard deviation" somewhere in its formula. It is like the recipe for "white sauce" in the cookbooks. You may skip it on the ground that you don't care for white sauce and want to get on to something more exotic, but you find that most of the recipes for other sauces begin, "First make some white sauce. Then. . . ."

There is a very simple way to find the standard deviation, proposed by W. L. Jenkins of Lehigh University, that will work well enough when you are in a hurry and when the distribution of scores is approximately "normal"—that is, when it resembles the familiar "bell-shaped curve." Subtract the sum of the bottom sixth of scores from the sum of the top sixth and divide by half the number of students tested:

$$\text{Standard deviation} = \frac{\text{Sum of high sixth} - \text{sum of low sixth}}{\text{Half the number of students}}$$

Let us try this formula on the following distribution of scores on a test of 40 items:

31 2	24 3	17 2
30 1	23 3	16 2
29 1	22 3	15 2
28 1	21 5	14 2
27 2	20 3	13 1
26 2	19 3	12 1
25 2	18 3	11 1

There are 45 students. A sixth of 45 is 7½ students. Ordinarily we would say "Forget about the half" or "Take the next higher number," but here the formula itself is an approximation; hence the numbers that go into it ought to be as nearly accurate as we can manage. While there would be no way to take half of the eighth student from the top, we can jolly well take half of his *score*. Hence we add the first seven scores down from the top and then add half of the eighth score. The sum of these is 216. Then we add the seven scores from the bottom plus half the eighth score. The sum of these is 102. Subtracting 102 from 216 gives us 114.

Now we have to divide 114 by half the number of students, which is 22.5. In the item-analysis, we left out that half student, since it would have been impossible to get half of him to sit with the highs and half with the lows. Here there is no point in leaving him out, since it is almost as easy to divide by 22.5 as it is to divide by 22. The quotient is 5.06, which rounds to 5 as the nearest whole number—the same as you would get in computing the standard deviation by orthodox procedures.

Now, the standard error of the average score on this test is the *standard deviation divided by the square root of the number of students.* (Since the number is above 30, we can forget about taking one less than the number of students.) The square root of 45 students is 6.7 students. (Don't bother to compute it; look it up in a table of square roots.) The standard deviation, 5, divided by 6.7 = 50.00 divided by 67 = .75 (rounding to the nearest hundredth).

Now you can see how the standard error of an average compares with the standard error of the scores that enter into it. Since this was a test of 40 items, the standard error of each score was approximately 3 raw-score points. The standard error of the average of the class now turns out to be only three-quarters of a point. This means that the chances are two out of three that the true average of the class on exactly this sort of test at the present time lies within .75 points of the average they got on this occasion (21.06 if you want to figure it out). The chances are 2 to 1 that it lies within 1.5 points: that is, that the true average lies between 19.56 and 22.56.

This ought to show you why it is still possible to find things out about education by means of tests even though the standard error of an individual score is quite large. Most of the time you are not dealing with individuals but with classes. You have not taught *Hamlet* in one way to Susie and in another way to Joe, but you may well have taught it in two different ways to two different classes of approximately equal ability (for example, by using the admirable Maynard Mack film in one class but not in the other). The average scores of the two classes on the same test may very well tell you whether the film made any *average* difference. Remember, however, that you must take the standard error of the *difference* between the two averages rather than the standard error of either average. This is computed exactly as the standard error of a difference was computed on page 13: square the standard errors of the two averages, add them, and take the square root.

Standard Error of a Difference Between Averages

We should like to run through this process once more using more orthodox procedures, since there are many situations in which the simple Jenkins formula will not work. Chief among these is the situation in which the distribution of scores does not look anything like the normal bell-shaped curve, as on a mastery test in which most of the scores are within a few points of a perfect score. Again, it is hard to apply to letter-grades, where the spread in scores is very small. Third, it may be difficult to apply, and entail large random errors, when the number of measures to be averaged is very small. We shall take up this case in the example below, since it will serve to illustrate the standard procedure with a minimum of numbers.

The problem arose when the writer and his friends were living in Chicago and had a choice between the Pennsylvania and the New York Central in getting to New York. Most of the men preferred the Central on the ground that it was smoother. Just to be ornery, the writer argued that they were the victims of propaganda: they had been reading the slogan "The Water-Level Route—You Can Sleep" for so many years that they had come to believe it. The writer argued that there was no true difference in bumpiness at all.

Since these were measurement men, they naturally cast about for some means of measuring bumpiness. One of them found an empty bottle that had contained Aqua Velva Shaving Lotion. It was admirable for the purpose, since it was a square bottle that could be held precisely in one position on its side, and it had a narrow mouth through which water would squirt rather than pour at every bump. They filled it half full of water—up to the point at which just no more water would spill out when the bottle was laid on its side. Then some tidy soul objected that they ought not to let the water spurt out on the floor of the car, or the porter might interrupt the experiment. This problem was solved when they got to Cleveland, which has a toy shop in the terminal. They bought a toy balloon and slipped it over the mouth of the bottle to catch the spilled water.

Then, when they all agreed that the train was going full speed, they laid the bottle on its side on the window-ledge of the car, pointing toward the aisle, so that it would make no difference whether the train was going uphill or downhill. They left it there five minutes and then took a reading to find out how much water had been displaced. (They had marked off a scale in millimeters on the side of the label.) After half an hour, when the train again was going full speed, they took another reading. There was time for only five readings before they went to bed. On the return trip, they changed tickets to the Pennsylvania and took five readings under exactly the same conditions. Since five dollars was riding on the outcome, they all checked every measure to make sure that there was no mistake and nothing unfair about the reading.

It turned out that the Central displaced an average of 9 millimeters of water per reading while the Pennsy displaced 14. This would have been enough for the average bet, but these were measurement men, so they insisted that the difference be significant at the 5% level or better before the bet would be paid. They quickly performed the necessary calculations on the back of an envelope and found that the difference was significant far beyond the 1% level. Hence there was less than one chance in a hundred that further readings, no matter how many times repeated, would finally average out to a verdict of "no real difference." How did they figure it?

The back of the envelope looked more or less like this:

Central

Score	f	d	fd	fd²
12	1	3	3	9
11	0	2	0	0
10	1	1	1	1
9	1	0	0	0
8	1	−1	−1	1
7	0	−2	0	0
6	1	−3	−3	9

N = 5. $\qquad$ 20, Σfd²

Pennsy

Score	f	d	fd	fd²
17	1	3	3	9
16	0	2	0	0
15	1	1	1	1
14	1	0	0	0
13	1	−1	−1	1
12	0	−2	0	0
11	1	−3	−3	9

N = 5. $\qquad$ 20, Σfd²

$\dfrac{20}{5} = 4. \ \sqrt{4} = 2$, S.D. or σ $\qquad$ $\dfrac{20}{5} = 4. \ \sqrt{4} = 2$, S.D. or σ

$$\text{S.E.} = \frac{\text{S.D.}}{\sqrt{N-1}} = \frac{2}{\sqrt{5-1}} = \frac{2}{\sqrt{4}} = \frac{2}{2} = 1, \text{ standard error of each average}$$

$$\text{S.E.}_{\text{diff.}} = \sqrt{1^2 + 1^2} = \sqrt{2} = 1.4, \text{ the standard error of the } \textit{difference.}$$

Of course, there is quite a lot to explain here, but the actual operations are as simple as falling off a log. After each score, you put down how many times it occurred under f (frequency). Here none of the scores occurred more than once, and scores of 11 and 7 on the Central, and of 16 and 12 on the Pennsy, did not occur at all, but we have entered them as 0 to make it clearer what we are doing in the column headed "d". Notice the numbers under d: in both railroads they go 3, 2, 1, 0, -1, -2, -3. What does that look like? It looks like these numbers tell how far away each score is from the middle score. That is why the column is headed d, standing for "deviations." The middle score does not deviate at all from itself, so its deviation is 0, and is so entered. You can always fill out the "d" column quite automatically, simply numbering up and down from the middle score. The next column is headed "fd," and what does that suggest from your memories of algebra? It suggests that you multiply each f by the corresponding d to get fd; and that is precisely what you do: you multiply the second column by the third to get the fourth. Then what does fd^2 suggest? It suggests that if you multiply the third column by the fourth, you will get the fifth—since d X fd = fd^2. Notice that wherever a zero enters into the multiplication, the product is zero, and notice that when you multiply two negative numbers together, as in columns three and four, the product is positive, as in column five. You add all those products in column five and write the sum at the bottom of the column. The rather odd symbol annexed to it, Σ, is the Greek capital S, and simply means "sum of." You divide this sum, 20, by the number of measures, 5, and get 4, the average *squared* deviation. The square root of $4 = 2$, which is the "standard deviation" of the scores for both the Central and the Pennsy, computed by orthodox and standard procedures that you can apply (with a little practice) to any distribution of test scores. For practice, you might apply it to the distribution of scores on page 19. The sum of the squared deviations (Σfd^2) in that case should come out to 1129. Dividing by N, 45, you get 25, and the square root of that is 5—the same as in the shorter Jenkins method.

The two lines of figures below the point at which we found the "standard deviations" of the two railroads should by now be familiar territory that we have traversed on foot. It will be good discipline for you to read every symbol in these two lines and make sure that you know why it is there. In the first of these lines, beginning S.E., what does the S.E. stand for? "Standard error," of course, as is written out at the end of the line. What kind of standard error is it? The standard error of an *average* of five scores, which means that we can use the formula: standard deviation of the measures divided by the square root of one less than the number of measures (page 18). We have found that the standard deviation of these measures is 2 (for both railroads). The number of measures in each case is 5. One less than this number is 4. The square root of 4 is 2. Hence the standard error of each average is 2 over 2, which is 1. See whether you can read all this in the single line of figures that begins "S.E."

Then, in the last line, $S.E._{diff.}$ pretty obviously stands for the standard error of the *difference* between these two averages: the square root of the sum of squares of the two separate standard errors. Since both have a standard error of 1, the square is also 1, and the sum of the two squares is 2. The square root of 2 (look it up!) is 1.4. The least that the two averages can differ, therefore, and have us certify it as a real difference at the 5% level, is 2.8 points (millimeters). If they differ by more than 3.6 points (2.6 times the standard error of the difference), we can certify it as "significant at the 1% level." Since the actual difference between the two averages was 5 points, it is obviously far and away beyond the 1% level: there is far less than one chance in a hundred that the obtained difference between the two averages was a fluke. Hence the measurers felt no compulsion to stay up all night on all subsequent trips between Chicago and New York, measuring the bumpiness of the two roads over every mile of roadbed. They had enough confidence in their statistical theory to realize that such effort would be wasted. There was considerably less than one chance in a hundred that any subsequent measurement of the same sort would ever upset the general verdict that "the Pennsy is bumpier than the Central between Chicago and New York."

Obviously such a conclusion would make the public relations officers of the Pennsy apoplectic with rage, and they might be tempted to spend fifty thousand dollars building some kind of go-cart to trail behind their trains in order to measure bumpiness with greater precision. But the whole theory of measurement suggests that such an investment would be unwise. When a difference gets out beyond the 1% level with even crude but fair measures, it is highly unlikely that refinement of the measures will show a true difference in the opposite direction.

We are now in a better position to appreciate what a "standard deviation" is. It is a kind of average of how far the scores are spread out from the middle score, or mean. One standard deviation above and one standard deviation below the mean will enclose two-thirds of the scores if the distribution is normal. Two above and two below will enclose 95% of the scores. This sounds exactly like the standard error—and, in fact, the two have the same basis in statistical theory. But notice that the standard error enclosed hypothetical scores: the limits within which scores might fall by pure chance in the selection of items if the same student were given an infinite number of parallel forms (without learning anything or forgetting anything). The standard deviation encloses the actual scores made by a given class in any one administration of the test or, in this case, the actual scores made by two different subjects in five administrations of the same test.

It is worth remembering that the standard deviation will usually lie between 10% and 20% of the number of items in the test, except in mastery tests in which most students come close to a perfect score, when it will be smaller. If you have to make a quick guess, probably the safest guess for most teacher-made tests (except mastery tests) is that the standard deviation will be 15% of the number of items in the test.

Since the actual scores made by a class will ordinarily spread out farther than the hypothetical scores that any individual might make on parallel forms, we must expect the standard deviation to be larger than the standard error of an individual test score. That is, in fact, what we found for the distribution of scores printed on page 19. The standard deviation of these scores was 5 raw-score points; the standard error of any individual score within this distribution was approximately 3 raw-score points; the standard error of a *difference* between any two of these scores was 4¼ points; and the standard error of the class average on this test was only .75 of one raw-score point. These figures will give you an idea of the relative order of size of the quantities we have been talking about up to this point.

Reliability

Test Reliability.

We are now in a position to compute the reliability of objective tests in which all items are given equal weight. It will take approximately two minutes after you know the standard deviation. (If the shortcut formula for the standard deviation escapes your memory, you will find it on page 19—but that is one you ought to learn by heart.) The reliability of the test depends on just three quantities: the number of items, the standard deviation, and the mean (average). If we use n for number of *items* (not number of students, remember!), s for the standard deviation, and M for the mean, the formula for computing the reliability of a test is the following:

$$\text{rel.} = 1 - \frac{M(n - M)}{ns^2} \qquad \text{(Kuder-Richardson Formula 21)}$$

In the scores printed on page 19, the mean was 21, the number of items was 40, and so the number of items minus the mean was 19. 21 X 19 = 399. In the denominator, n was 40 and the square of the standard deviation was 25. 40 X 25 = 1,000. Rounding a bit, we get 400 over 1,000 or .4. Then—do not forget this—we subtract .4 from 1 and get .6 (or .60, if that looks more familiar) as the reliability of the test.

If even this much computation leaves you cold, you can find the approximate reliability of most of your tests in one of the two tables below. If the average score on your test is between 70% and 90% correct, use the

first table. If it is between 50% and 70% correct, use the
second table. Then compute the standard deviation of
your test by the shortcut formula on page 19. If the
standard deviation (labeled S.D. in the tables) is nearest
to 10% of the items, use line 1; if 15%, use line 2; if 20%
(which happens very rarely), use line 3. If you have to
guess, use line 2. Then choose the column that is nearest
to the number of items in your test. The figure at the
intersection of this row and column will be the
approximate reliability of your test.

Approximate Reliability of Easy Tests
(average 70% to 90% correct)

Number of items (n)	20	30	40	50	60	70	80	90	100
If S.D. is .10n		.21	.48	.62	.69	.75	.78	.81	.83	.85
If S.D. is .15n		.68	.80	.84	.88	.90	.91	.92	.93	.94
If S.D. is .20n		.84	.90	.92	.94	.95	.96	.96	.97	.97

Approximate Reliability of Hard Tests
(average 50% to 70% correct)

Number of items (n)	20	30	40	50	60	70	80	90	100
If S.D. is .10n			.21	.41	.53	.61	.66	.71	.74	.77
If S.D. is .15n		.49	.67	.75	.80	.84	.86	.88	.89	.90
If S.D. is .20n		.74	.83	.87	.90	.92	.93	.94	.94	.95

These reliability coefficients are conservative estimates of the correlation you would get if you
administered two parallel forms of the test so closely
together that no learning took place between them and
computed the correlation between the two sets of
scores. In simpler terms, test reliability is an estimate of
how close you would come to the same set of scores if
you gave a parallel form of the test. It is not a per cent
and should never be referred to as "a reliability of
60%," or "60% reliable."

Note the decisive effect of the standard deviation—
because it is in the denominator of the reliability
formula and squared. A large number in the denominator at this point will make a smaller quantity to be
subtracted from 1 and hence leave a larger reliability.
The number of items, n, also in the denominator, has a
similar effect. The location of the mean, M, in the

numerator may seem to give an advantage to easy tests, but this is more than offset by the fact that such tests generally have a smaller standard deviation.

We are often asked what level of reliability is satisfactory. The answer has to be "whatever you can get in a given field within given time limits." Test publishers have traditionally not been satisfied with reliabilities less than .90, but teacher-made tests must usually settle for less. Over 300 teachers have attended the writer's classes in measurement, and most of these have produced tests and tried them out in their own classes. Most of those that the writer regarded as good, usable tests achieved reliabilites between .60 and .80. If we wanted a test to be highly reliable to serve as a final examination, we usually found that it took two class periods and had to be administered on two successive days: Part I on Thursday, for example, and Part II on Friday.

It is good to compute these reliabilities routinely because they take only about two minutes apiece and flash a warning signal when the reliability dips so low (as a rough rule-of-thumb, below .60) that the scores are hardly worth recording. They will also set you up in the eyes of your colleagues as a man of science, since one of the few terms in testing they have heard about is "reliability." They vaguely believe that it takes vast erudition and possibly an electronic computer to compute reliability, and they will be greatly impressed if you can do it in two minutes for any of your tests on the back of an envelope. Still, you must not let them go away with the idea that reliability is the only virtue in a test. The easiest way to achieve it would be to ask a large number of petty factual questions in a form that could be answered very rapidly, so that you might get 100 answers from each student within one class period. They would probably hit a reliability of .90, and since the brighter and better students would probably get higher scores than the dull and lazy, the scores might have quite a respectable correlation with your grades. Still, you would know, your colleagues would know, and your students would know that it was a lousy test. The thing to do, therefore, is to make the best test you can within the time-limits you have available and *then* compute the reliability. If it is unsatisfactory, it only means that you need more items to work up to a stable score; hence make another test. The following formula will tell you how many times to lengthen the test to get up to any desired reliability:

$$\frac{\text{(The reliability you want)} \times \text{(1 - the reliability you got)}}{\text{(The reliability you got)} \times \text{(1 - the reliability you want)}}$$

If you want .90 and got .60 with your first test, this becomes:

$$\frac{.90 \times (1 - .60)}{.60 \times (1 - .90)} = \frac{.90 \times .40}{.60 \times .10} = \frac{.3600}{.0600} = 6 \text{ (times longer)}$$

Thus, it takes 6 tests with a reliability of .60 to work up to a reliability of .90. Also, it takes 3 tests with a reliability of .75 to work up to a reliability of .90. Either of these is entirely feasible if you have the students for a semester or for a year. Simply make up more tests of the same ability.

This formula seems inconsistent with the effect of the standard deviation—the spread of scores—on reliability, and to make reliability entirely a function of the number of items in the test. The supposed inconsistency can be straightened out as follows. Suppose you have just given a test on appreciation of *Hamlet* to your Advanced Placement Class of superior students, and its reliability with this class turns out to be .60. That means that if you gave another test of the same kind to the same class tomorrow, quite a few students would change position enough to affect their grade. There are two ways in which you could increase this reliability. One would be to go across the hall and administer the same test to a regular, unselected class that had everybody in it from geniuses to morons. The reliability over there might well go up to .90, since these people differed so widely in ability that another test of the same kind would not shift the rank-order of very many students. This one test would be sufficient to give *that* class reliable grades on *Hamlet*. "But," you would properly argue, "I am not responsible for the grades of the class across the hall; I am responsible for the grades of this particular class; and I want them to be sufficiently reliable so that one more test would not shift them in very many instances." Hence you apply the foregoing formula and find out that you would have to give six tests of this kind to this particular class during the unit on *Hamlet* to get *their* scores up to a reliability of .90. The formula applies only to the sort of group that you have just tested, and it assumes that the range of ability within this group is not going to change appreciably during those six tests. For this reason, the reliability can be predicted on the basis of number of items alone, assuming that the true standard deviation within this group is going to remain constant.

We must not forget the lesson of our first section: that reliability can be increased (per unit of testing time) by dropping or touching up items that proved to be too hard, too easy, or non-discriminating. This, also, is not inconsistent with the formula for lengthening the test. That formula merely says, "Given the kinds of items you have now, it will take X times more items to boost reliability to .90." But if you drop hopeless items and improve others, the desired reliability may well be attained with fewer items than the formula predicts.

Correlation

This is the other magic word from the art and mystery of testing. If you can do both reliabilities *and* correlations and come up with results within five minutes, your colleagues will regard you as another Einstein. Actually, any moderately bright eighth grader who has been getting B's in arithmetic can learn how to do the simpler kind of correlation in about fifteen minutes, and it should not take him longer than five minutes to compute one for a class of average size.

Here's how to do it: find the percentage of students who stood in the top half of the group on *both* measures you are correlating and look up the correlation (r) corresponding to this percentage in the following table:

%	r	%	r	%	r	%	r	%	r
45	.95	37	.69	29	.25	21	−.25	13	−.69
44	.93	36	.65	28	.19	20	−.31	12	−.73
43	.91	35	.60	27	.13	19	−.37	11	−.77
42	.88	34	.55	26	.07	18	−.43	10	−.81
41	.85	33	.49	25	.00	17	−.49	9	−.85
40	.81	32	.43	24	−.07	16	−.55	8	−.88
39	.77	31	.37	23	−.13	15	−.60	7	−.91
38	.73	30	.31	22	−.19	14	−.65	6	−.93

These are called "tetrachoric correlations," while the more common but more difficult kind are called "product-moment correlations." They mean the same thing, in the sense that the tetrachoric yields a fairly accurate estimate of the correlation that you would get by the product-moment method. Tetrachorics are perfectly respectable and are often used in educational research, but you can see that they are not very precise, since a difference of 1% can make a difference as great as .07 in the correlation. However, the reliability of the data that teachers usually have to work with and the relatively small numbers of students involved usually do not justify more precise methods of computation. The best you can hope to get by any method is a rough idea of the general order of magnitude of the relationship.

Since even 1% of the students can make so much difference in the correlation, it is important to use a standard, uniform method of counting how many students stood in the top half on each measure. We trust that you know how to find the middle score on each measure. List the scores on each measure from highest to lowest and put a tally after each score for each student who made it. After all the scores have been tallied, count down the tallies to half the number of students in the group. The score at which this middle tally falls is the middle score.

You will ordinarily have the students listed in alphabetical order, and after each name you will have the two scores that you are correlating. After you have found the middle score on each measure, go down the list and put a check after each score that stands *above* the middle score on that measure; a straight line after each score that stands *at* the middle score. Do this separately for each of the two measures.

Then, if you need three more students with middle scores on Measure A to take in half of the group, put a check through the first three straight lines on Measure A that you come to in alphabetical order. If you need five more students with middle scores on Measure B, put a check through the first five straight lines after the scores on that measure. Then count how many students have *two* checks after their names. Turn this number into a percent by dividing it by the *total* number of students (not by the number in the top half). Look up this per cent in the foregoing table. The decimal corresponding to it will be the correlation between the two measures.

It is not necessary for the two measures to be on anything like the same scale. It is perfectly valid, for example, to correlate height in inches with weight in pounds; or scores on an objective test that run from 200 to 800 with scores on an essay that run from 1 to 9. All that is necessary is to count how many students stood in the top half of this same group on *both* measures.

It is impossible and meaningless, however, to correlate the scores of two different groups on the same measure: for example, to correlate the scores of the boys with those of the girls. You start with a single list of names, each of which has two scores after it. Then you can correlate the first set of scores with the second set of scores. But if you have two separate lists of names, each with a single score after it, there is no way to count how many students who stood high on the first measure also stood high on the second. There is only one measure.

Teachers often speak loosely of "correlating" one class with another when they really mean "comparing." They use the longer term only because it sounds more scientific *to them*; but to anyone who knows what a correlation means, it is the most flagrant of boners. There is no way to correlate two groups of students on the same measure; one can only correlate two sets of measures on the same students. To compare the performance of two groups of students on the same test or other measure, you compare their averages, and if you want to find out whether the averages were "really" different, you compute the standard errors of these averages and then the standard error of the difference, as we explained on pages 18—25.

The general meaning of correlation may be remembered this way. A positive correlation means that the higher a student stood on one measure, the higher he stood on the other. A negative correlation means that the higher he stood on one measure, the *lower* he stood on the other. (We often get such correlations: for example, between number of errors in a composition and teachers' grades on those compositions.) A zero or near-zero correlation (roughly from .25 to —.25) means that a student who stood high on one measure might stand anywhere at all on the other (for example, the correlation between height and I.Q.).

The topic of correlation is closely related to the preceding topic of reliability, because often the only way of computing the reliability of a test is to give two tests of the same ability and correlate the two sets of scores. This is true of (a) essay tests and (b) tests in which the items receive different numbers of points. The Kuder-Richardson Formula 21 given on page 26 will work only for objective tests in which all items are scored either 1 or 0: that is, as either right or not-right (wrongs and omits counting equally as not-right). It is also true (although this principle is often violated) of tests in which more than 20% of the students were unable to finish: that is, of *speeded* tests. Speed spuriously increases reliability to an extent that, if the less able students were able to finish only half the test, it would be almost impossible to get a low reliability. Yet sometimes it is appropriate and necessary to give a speeded test. In such cases, the only fair, acceptable way to estimate reliability is to give two tests of the same sort and compute the correlation between the two sets of scores.

Sometimes teachers cheat themselves by securing two essays, each graded independently, for their final examination; by correlating grades on the first set of essays with grades on the second set; and by calling that correlation the reliability of the examination. It is not;

it is the reliability of *one* essay. If you use the sum or average of both essay grades as the grade for the examination, its reliability is twice the correlation divided by one plus the correlation. For example, if the correlation is .60,

$$\text{rel.} = \frac{2 \times .60}{1 + .60} = \frac{1.20}{1.60} = \frac{12}{16} = \frac{3}{4} = .75$$

This is called the "Spearman-Brown Prophecy Formula." Another form of it appears on page 28. It should also be used whenever you are computing reliabilities by the old method of correlating scores on even-numbered items with scores on odd-numbered items. The correlation you get is the reliability of *half* the test. To get the reliability of the whole test, do as above: double the correlation and divide by one plus that correlation.

III. Standardized Testing

11. Evaluation and Interpretation of Tests

Albert E. Bartz

Finally we have come to the point where we can devote a full discussion to the construction and interpretation of tests. The previous chapters have given us the necessary information and tools to discuss tests intelligently. In this chapter we will consider two important characteristics of an adequate test: reliability and validity.

RELIABILITY

One of the questions that confronts us when we must choose a test for some testing purpose is: "Is this test reliable?" *By reliability, we mean that a test tests consistently and accurately.* If we give a test one time and it gives us certain results, and at a second administration gives us a totally different result, which test are we to believe? This test is not reliable. That is, it is not testing consistently and accurately. If a test is not reliable, we do not know whether Individual A who scored in the middle of the distribution actually belongs at the top or the bottom. In other words, there would have not been much point in giving the test in the first place. If the object of a test is to separate individuals on the basis of some certain trait, we do not know if we have accomplished any separation if our test is not reliable.

An important consideration, then, is determining whether or not a test is reliable. How might we do this? The most straight forward way would be to use a method of correlation. If we obtain a high positive correlation between two administrations of the same test to the same people, our test must be testing consistently, since the high coefficient means a high degree of relationship. If several individuals scored high on one administration and low on the other, the relationship would be lower, and the reliability less. When a test is reliable, the scores made by the members of the group will be consistent from one administration to the next. A reliable test, therefore, is relatively free of chance errors of measurement and scores earned on it are stable and trustworthy.

There are three ways in which we can determine the reliability of a test. They are the Test-Retest Method, Alternate Forms Method and Split-Half Method.

Test—Retest Method

The simplest and most straight forward method for determining reliability would be to give the test twice to the same individuals. We would then use one of the methods of correlation described in the preceding chapter to determine the relationship of the two administrations. As was mentioned before, the coefficient of correlation yielded by this method would be the relationship of how the individuals performed on the two tests. If the relationship is high, the test is testing consistently and is reliable.

However, there are various objections to this method. If a test is repeated within a short time interval, many individuals would be certain to recall answers that they had given previously, and thus spend their time on the difficult material. This would increase some scores and the correlation coefficient would not be an accurate estimate of the relationship. The type of test would, of course, affect the amount of transfer from one administration to the next.

If the test is repeated after a long time interval, growth and maturity (especially if the subjects are children) would affect the performance on the second administration. Certain experiences by different individuals during this interval might influence their perfromance also. Because of the difficulty of controlling these varying conditions, the Test-Retest Method is used less frequently than the other two.

ALTERNATE FORMS METHOD

An obvious way to eliminate the objections to the Test-Retest Method would be to give a different test at the second administration. Then there would be no memory factor to increase the scores of some individuals. This different test for the second administration must be very similar to the first test if our reliability coefficient is to be meaningful. Let us denote these alternate forms as Form A and Form B.

However, it would be necessary to construct an Alternate Form B for every test for which we wanted to determine the reliability coefficient. Many times this is not feasible because of the amount of time and work involved. When accurate alternate forms are constructed, the reliability coefficient yielded is relatively accurate.

SPLIT–HALF METHOD

Perhaps the easiest method for determining the reliability of a test is by the Split-Half Method. In this method the test is broken down into two parts, and a correlation coefficient is obtained between the two parts of the test. The most often used method for dividing the test into two parts is the odd and even method. In this way, each individual has two scores, a score on the odd numbered items in a test, and a score on the even items. It is necessary to go through the answer sheet for each individual and tabulate the number of right on the odd numbered items and the number right on the even numbered items. These scores are tabulated in the X and Y column of the Pearson product-moment table such as in Table 21. In essence, we are treating the two halves as separate tests. The tabulation for one individual might be:

Individual	Total Score	Odd numbered items correct	Even numbered items correct	X (odd)	Y (even)
A	32	17	15	17	15

We would do this for each individual in the test until we had a table similar to the one of Table 21. The coefficient yielded by this method would be the relationship of the two halves of the test. However, we want a coefficient that gives us the reliability of the entire test. It is necessary to substitute in the following formula (Spearman-Brown Prophecy Formula).

$$r_t = \frac{2r_{oe}}{1 + r_{oe}}$$

r_t = reliability coefficient of entire test

r_{oe} = coefficient of correlation between the two halves

The r_t is the reliability coefficient of the entire test. Let us consider an example using this method for finding the reliability of a test.

TABLE 21
Illustration of Split Half Method
of Correlation

Individual	X(odd)	Y(even)	x	y	x^2	y^2	xy
A	12	10	1	0	1	0	0
B	10	8	−1	−2	1	4	2
C	9	11	−2	1	4	1	−2
D	14	11	3	1	9	1	3
E	13	10	2	0	4	0	0
F	8	8	−3	−2	9	4	6
G	12	11	1	1	1	1	1
H	11	10	0	0	0	0	0
I	11	11	0	1	0	1	0
J	10	10	−1	0	1	0	0
	110	100	0	0	30	12	10

SUMMARY

$$M_x = 11$$

$$M_y = 10$$

$$\Sigma x^2 = 30$$

$$\Sigma y^2 = 12$$

$$\Sigma xy = 10$$

$$r_{oe} = \frac{\Sigma xy}{\sqrt{(\Sigma x^2)(\Sigma y^2)}}$$

$$= \frac{10}{\sqrt{(30)(12)}}$$

$$= \frac{10}{\sqrt{360}}$$

$$= \frac{10}{19}$$

$$r_{oe} = .53 \text{ (app.)}$$

The steps in determining the reliability of the split-half test are the same as in the general procedure for determining the Pearson product-moment r. However, the coefficient yielded is based on one-half of the test. To find the reliability of the entire test, it is necessary to substitute in the Spearman-Brown prophecy formula.

The reliability of the entire test is given by:

$$r_t = \frac{2r_{oe}}{1 + r_{oe}}$$

$$= \frac{2(.53)}{1 + .53}$$

$$= \frac{1.06}{1.53}$$

$$r_t = .69 \text{ (app.)}$$

This gives the reliability coefficient for the entire test.

We have seen in the last few paragraphs how we can estimate the reliability using the Split-Half Method of correlation. What is the rationale for this method? The Test-Retest and the Alternate Form methods were straight forward in that if reliability is present an individual will make comparable scores in regard to the rest of the group on both administrations. Is there similar reasoning behind the Split-Half method?

When we separate an individual's total score into odd and even correct, we would expect him to do equally well on the odd and even items (if odd and even items are matched for difficulty). If this is the case, the test is reliable, i.e., it is measuring consistently. If he does not do equally well, the test is not measuring consistently and therefore is not reliable. However, this split-half coefficient is not the same thing as the coefficients obtained by the Alternate Form or Test-Retest methods. It measures internal consistency and not consistency from administration to administration. Whenever the reliability coefficient is cited in reports and articles, it is usually identified by the method used to obtain it.

THE STANDARD ERROR OF MEASUREMENT

When we review the results of a test, how much confidence can we place in our score? In other words, how accurate are our scores? Suppose that Individual A made a score of 79. How much confidence do we have that our test is measuring accurately and that 79 is the individual's true score? By the true score we refer to the score that the test would give if there were no errors present in determining his score. We may represent this by the formula:

$$X_T = X - X_E$$
$$\text{where } X_T = \text{``true'' score}$$
$$X = \text{obtained score}$$
$$X_E = \text{``error'' score}$$

It is obvious that the confidence we can place in a score depends on the gap between the obtained score and the true score. If the difference between the true and obtained score is small, we can be quite confident that the obtained score is a good measure of the individual's performance. However, if the difference is large, i.e., there is a great discrepancy between the obtained and true scores, our test has given us a faulty measurement.

Unfortunately, our test scores are obtained scores and we have no idea of just exactly what the true score for any individual might be. There is a way in which we can determine to a certain extent how much a score might deviate from a true value. This is commonly called the Standard Error of Measurement. The formula is

$$SE = SD \sqrt{1 - r_t}$$

where

SD = standard deviation of the distribution

r_t = reliability coefficient of the test.

We use the Standard Error of Measurement to determine the range in which the true score of an individual probably lies. If the obtained score of an individual is 75 and the Standard Error of Measurement is 5, we can say that two out of three times his obtained score does not differ from his true score more than ±5. In two out of three times his true score would actually fall between 70 and 80.

Let us consider an example. Suppose that the SD of a test is 10 and the reliability coefficient is .84. By the above formula the Standard Error of Measurement is

$$SE = SD \sqrt{1 - r_t}$$
$$= 10 \sqrt{1 - .84}$$
$$= 10 \sqrt{.16}$$
$$= 10 \ (.4)$$
$$SE = 4$$

Thus the odds are two to one that the obtained score of any individual does not differ from his true score by ±4. If Individual A had a score of 79, we may feel confident that his true score actually lies in the range from 75 to 83.

The main purpose in testing is to separate individuals in respect to the trait that we are testing. You have probably inferred by now that two different scores made by two individuals does not necessarily mean they are different in respect to the trait being measured. Suppose that one makes a score of 75 and another a score of 78, and the Standard Error of Measurement is 4. The range for the first individual is 75 ±4, or 71 to 79, and for the second individual 78 ±4, or 74 to 82. Has our test done any separating? We cannot be sure on scores that are close together within the limits of the Standard Error of Measurement. If there is an overlap in the range, such as in the above example, we cannot be sure that the true scores of the individuals are actually different. It is obvious that the smaller the Standard Error of Measurement the more accurate our obtained scores.

We should notice from the formula

$$SE = SD \sqrt{1 - r_t}$$

that the reliability of the test is important in determining the size of the Standard Error of Measurement. If r_t is perfect, or 1.0, the term under the radical reduces to zero, and the Standard Error of Measurement is now zero. If r_t is zero the Standard Error becomes the same as the SD. We can see from this that the higher the reliability of the test, the smaller the Standard Error of Measurement.

VALIDITY

As was mentioned earlier in this chapter, one of the necessary requirements for a good test is validity. By validity we mean that a test is testing what it is supposed to test. If we construct a test to measure mathematical achievement and it turns out as a better measure of ability in cake-baking it has little validity. To be valid a test must serve the purpose for which it is intended.

A test can be highly reliable, but not valid. In the somewhat exaggerated example above, our test may be highly reliable (i.e., give consistent results) but it certainly is not valid. It is not testing what it is supposed to test.

We may determine the validity of a test by calculating the validity coefficient. To do this, we use our well known method of correlation between two tests and the correlation coefficient is our validity coefficient.

What other tests do we use to determine our coefficient? The usual procedure is to choose some other test that is well known as a good test for the purpose for which our test is intended. The test is known as the criterion. If we construct a test to determine intelligence, we want it to correlate highly with a well-known test in this area. Our criterion might be the Wechsler-Bellevue or the Stanford-Binet. If the relationship is good, i.e., the validity coefficient is high, our test must be testing the same thing as the criterion.

It should be obvious by now that a test is worthless if it is not valid. If the validity of a test we have constructed is low, we must consider improving it or discarding it altogether.

Once the criterion is selected, it is a straight forward procedure to determine a validity coefficient. We need only to administer the two different tests to a group and find the correlation coefficient between the two tests. If the relationship is good, the coefficient is high, and our test is highly valid. If the relationship is poor, the coefficient is low, and our test is not valid. An illustration of the computation of the validity coefficient is shown in Table 22. Let us say that Test X is a test that we constructed for determining ability in arithmetic. The criterion is Test Y, a standardized test for arithmetic ability. To find the correlation we use the Pearson product-moment method.

TABLE 22
Calculation of a Validity Coefficient

Individual	X	Y	x	y	x^2	y^2	xy
A	14	24	1	3	1	9	3
B	16	23	3	2	9	4	6
C	17	25	4	4	16	16	16
D	13	21	0	0	0	0	0
E	13	20	0	−1	0	1	0
F	14	23	1	2	1	4	2
G	14	23	1	2	1	4	2
H	10	18	−3	−3	9	9	9
I	9	17	−4	−4	16	16	16
J	10	16	−3	−5	9	25	15
	130	210	0	0	62	88	69

SUMMARY

$$M_x = 13$$

$$M_y = 21$$

$$\Sigma x^2 = 62$$

$$\Sigma y^2 = 88$$

$$\Sigma xy = 69$$

$$r = \frac{\Sigma xy}{\sqrt{(\Sigma x^2)(\Sigma y^2)}}$$

$$= \frac{69}{\sqrt{(62)(88)}}$$

$$= \frac{69}{\sqrt{5456}}$$

$$= \frac{69}{74}$$

$$r = .93 \text{ (app.)}$$

Since the correlation is high, we will assume that our test is measuring the same thing as the criterion.

In determining the validity, it is necessary that the reliability coefficient of both tests be high. This is a matter of common sense, since our validity coefficient is meaningless if either of the tests is not reliable. A validity coefficient of .93 is very high. Usually validity coefficients are of the order of .60 to .70.

How large must the validity coefficient be before we can infer that our test is valid? This will depend on the type of test. For a discussion of the different size validity coefficients for various tests the reader is referred to any standard text in statistics.

THE USE OF STANDARDIZED TESTS

The classroom teacher often finds himself faced with the administration of one or more standardized tests to his pupils at least once during the school year. It is usually difficult if not impossible for many schools to have the service of a trained test technician to handle the testing program. As a result, the administration and interpretation of the tests is left to the teacher. Some teachers begrudgingly administer the test, and, because of their feelings of inadequacy and lack of confidence in test practices, fail to make full use of the information given by the scores. On the other hand, some with a flair for testing will plunge into an intensive testing program and make all sorts of unqualified conclusions and assumptions based on the test scores.

With a growing emphasis on the use of standardized tests, the future teacher needs to have a middle of the road approach. He has to be confident in his testing and evaluation, but, at the same time, cautious and conservative in his use and interpretations. This, as with anything else, is established through practice and constant use.

As was mentioned previously, a standardized test is one that has been administered to a selected sample, and norms have been constructed on the basis of these scores.

A teacher-made test is usually considered non-standardized because it is written for the sole purpose of discrimination of achievement for one class. However, many standardized tests were at one time teacher-made tests, but with constant refinement were finally administered to a sample of students, norms were constructed, and the test was printed and put on the market.

The reader will note in the preceding paragraph the repetition of the term *sampling*. This forms the important first rule in the use of standardized tests: *the test that is being used should have norms based on a sample that is very much like the test group.* Otherwise, the scores made by the group will not be comparable when placed on the norms for the standardized test. The manual accompanying the test usually gives the information as to the nature of the sample.

Of course, many tests will not be based on a sample that is *exactly* like the group to be tested. In this case the teacher must use a certain amount of discretion in interpreting the scores. If the group to be tested is made up of pupils in a small high school in Minnesota and the test norms are based on a sample from large high schools in another state, certain allowances will have to be made.

The second rule concerns the purpose of the test. In most situations the school administration selects the test and the teacher has only the responsibility of giving the test. However, if the teacher has the freedom to select the test, *the test must be one that is going to measure what the teacher wants.* This may sound like a very low level of common sense, but the title of a test is not always indicative of its purpose. Reference should always be made to a catalog of tests that lists the information concerning the purpose of the test. If the teacher is still in doubt, most publishers offer a specimen set which contains several copies of the test, a scoring key, and instruction manual.

The third rule incorporates many smaller ones. *Follow the instruction manual carefully.* The purpose of the manual is to make the test situation as similar as possible to that of the original sample upon which the norms were based. If the norms are to be accurate, the test situations must be similar. The test manual includes instructions on how to administer the test, instructions to the examinees, time limits for the various sections of the test, and directions for plotting a profile chart of each student and the interpretation of these charts. Since each test is different these points will not be taken up individually. However, it cannot be overemphasized that the manual must be followed carefully.

SUMMARY

It must be remembered that standardized tests, like all others, are subject to certain limitations. Generally speaking, the Standard Error of Measurement is usually less for standardized tests than for teacher-made tests. However, the interpretation of test scores must take into account motivation, emotional level, and other factors that influence test scores. It can be seen that a test score is just a sample of an individual's performance. With repeated testing, the average score on these repetitions would be indicative of his performance in the long run, but a test is administered only once. His score may be too high, too low, or just right. As a result, a test score should not be considered absolute, but should be interpreted with reference to other factors.

It cannot be overemphasized that the results of a single test should be viewed with caution. Too many students have been wrongly advised against going to college, placed in the wrong ability group, etc., simply on the basis of a single test score. Cumulative records, grades, confidential reports, and other test results should be interpreted as a meaningful whole. Attaching too much inportance to a single test score is the mark of a novice.

12. Aptitude, Intelligence and Achievement

Alexander G. Wesman

Which is more helpful—an aptitude test or an achievement test?—a general mental ability test or a differential aptitude test battery? There are purposes for which each kind of test is superior; there are circumstances in which all are useful; there are conditions when any one of these types may be pressed into service to yield information ordinarily obtained from another type of test. What are these purposes, circumstances and conditions? When should an achievement test be used rather than an intelligence test, or an aptitude test? What advantages do multiple-score aptitude batteries have over single-score intelligence tests?

As a preliminary, let us look at the basic characteristics of achievement tests, intelligence tests and aptitude tests. By definition, an achievement test measures what the examinee has learned. But an intelligence test measures what the examinee has learned. And an aptitude test measures what the examinee has learned. So far, no difference is revealed. Yet three of the traditional categories into which tests are classified are intelligence, aptitude and achievement. Now these categories are very handy; they permit publishers to divide their catalogs into logical segments, and provide textbook authors with convenient chapter headings. Unfortunately, the categories represent so much oversimplification as to cause confusion as to what is being

From *Test Service Bulletin,* Number 51, 1956, by Alexander G. Wesman. Reprinted with consent of the Psychological Corporation, New York.

measured. What all three kinds of tests measure is what the subject has learned. The ability to answer a proverbs item is no more a part of the examinee's heredity than is the ability to respond to an item in a mechanical comprehension test or in a social studies test. All are learned behavior.

Moreover, all are intelligent behavior. It takes intelligence to supply the missing number in a number series problem. It also requires intelligence to figure out which pulley will be most efficient, or to remember which president proposed an inter-American doctrine. We can say, then, that an intelligence test measures intelligent behavior, an aptitude test measures intelligent behavior and an achievement test measures intelligent behavior.

Finally, all three types of tests measure probability of future learning or performance, which is what we generally mean when we speak of "aptitude." In business and industry, the chances that an employee will profit from training or will perform new duties capably may be predicted by scores on an intelligence test, by scores on one or more specific aptitude tests, or by some measure of the degree of skill the employee already possesses. Similarly, test users in the schools know that an intelligence test is usually a good instrument for predicting English grades, a social studies test is often helpful for prediction of future grades in social studies, and a mechanical comprehension test is likely to be useful in predicting for scientific or technical courses. So, intelligence tests are aptitude tests, achievement tests are aptitude tests and aptitude tests are aptitude tests.

Content—What the Test Covers

On what basis are the types to be differentiated? One possible basis is that of content. Quite often, we can look at the subject matter of a test and classify the test as achievement or intelligence or aptitude. But content is not a sure guide by any means.

Let us take a specific item. A student is taught to multiply $(x-y)$ by (x). If he demonstrates that he can perform this operation correctly, we accept this item as an achievement measure. Next, without specific formal instruction, he is asked to multiply (p+q) by (p−q), and again answers correctly. Is this achievement? The mathematics teacher would say it is. Is it aptitude? Certainly the ability to perceive the analogy between the taught and untaught algebraic problems is indicative of future learning ability in algebra. Is it intelligence? The demonstrated ability to generalize is clearly symptomatic of intelligence.

The same point can be made with regard to entire subtests. In the *Metropolitan Achievement* series there is a Spelling test; one of the *Differential Aptitude Tests* is also a test called Spelling. Tests of arithmetic comprehension may be found in most achievement batteries; one of the subtests in each of the *Wechsler Intelligence Scales* measures arithmetic comprehension. What does all this mean? Have we demonstrated that the authors of these tests are confused, or is our classification system less neat and simple than it appears to be on the surface?

We believe the classification system is at fault. The teacher who has taught pupils how to solve arithmetic problems is perfectly justified in claiming that the pupils' performance on tests in these abilities represents achievement—both hers and theirs. At the same time, the learning of the skills and appreciations by the pupils is evidence of intelligence. Furthermore, the possession of the skills and of the ability to learn demonstrates the possession of aptitude for further learning in those same school subjects, and probably in other subjects as well. For example, scores on the *DAT* Spelling Test provide excellent prediction of success in learning stenography.

Process—What the Examinee Has To Do

It would appear, then, that test content is not entirely adequate to discriminate among intelligence, achievement and aptitude testing. Can we use process to discriminate among them? Shall we say that achievement is measured when the subject is tested for recall of what he has been taught, and that intelligence is shown in the ability to generalize from the facts?

Every modern educator and every modern test constructor would reject such classification outright.

Rare is the teacher who will admit her students are merely memorizing facts; rare is the curriculum which is not aimed at developing the ability to generalize, to apply learned principles in new situations. Furthermore, inspection of the items in some of our most highly regarded intelligence tests will reveal many items which are as direct questions of fact as any to be found in the least imaginative achievement tests. Processes of recognition, recall and rote repetition may be distinguishable from processes of generalization, appreciation, and problem solving—but apparently they are not satisfactory for distinguishing between intelligence and achievement.

Function—How the Test Results Are Used

If test content will not serve, nor test process, what will successfully discriminate intelligence or aptitude from achievement measures? A logical candidate would seem to be function. What are we trying to accomplish with the test scores? How are the results to be used? What inferences are to be drawn concerning the examinee? If a test's function is to record present or past accomplishment, what is measured may be called achievement. If we wish to make inferences concerning future learning, what is measured is thought of as aptitude. One kind of aptitude test, usually some combination of verbal and numerical and/or abstract reasoning measures, is sometimes called an intelligence test; more properly, in educational settings, it is called a scholastic aptitude test.

In educational testing . . .

If the purpose is to evaluate the effectiveness of teaching or training, and the test is designed to measure what has been specifically taught, we have an achievement situation. The more closely the test reflects what has been taught, the better it suits the purpose. The statement holds equally well if the intent is to grade students on the basis of what they have learned in a course. If, in addition, we wish to infer how well a student will learn in the future, we have an aptitude situation. The greater the similarity between what has been learned and what is to be learned, the better the achievement test suits the aptitude purpose. A test of achievement in first term algebra is likely to be an excellent test of aptitude for second term algebra. On the other hand, such a test is likely to predict less well future course grades in physics, French and shop. Nor can an achievement test in algebra be used effectively to predict course grades before the students have been exposed to algebra. Some other measure of aptitude is required.

If we are interested only in predicting algebra grades, a numerical aptitude test is likely to prove best. The chances are, however, that we are also interested in predicting success in other subjects at the same time. In that case, we have several choices. We can select achievement tests in as many relevant or nearly relevant subjects as are available, and use these tests as predictors. This approach will obviously be most effective where past and future courses are most alike; it will be least effective where past and future courses are least alike. Concretely, achievement tests can function as aptitude measures best in the early school years, less well at the junior and senior high school levels where courses become increasingly differentiated.

Another possible choice for predicting success in various courses is the scholastic aptitude or so-called group intelligence test. To the extent that various courses demand verbal and/or numerical facility for successful learning, a test which measures those aptitudes will probably prove useful. Again, this verbal-numerical ability is likely to play a more pervasive role in the elementary grade subjects than in the high school. Even at the high school level, grades are so often affected by the student's verbal expression that scholastic aptitude tests often correlate well with those grades even in subjects such as mechanical drawing and music. In such courses when grades are assigned on the basis of what the student can *do,* rather than how well he can speak or write about it, the predictive value of verbal or verbal-numerical aptitude tests is likely to be less.

A third alternative is the use of differential aptitude test batteries. These batteries ordinarily include measures of verbal and numerical aptitude, just as the scholastic aptitude intelligence tests do; they also provide measures of other aptitudes as well—spatial, mechanical, clerical, and the like. The instruments yield a set of scores which recognize intra-individual differences, accepting the fact that a student may be fairly high in verbal ability, average in numerical, very high in mechanical aptitude, and very poor in clerical speed and accuracy. These multi-score batteries provide broader coverage of mental functioning than is obtainable from the more limited scholastic aptitude test.

Is this broader coverage worth the effort? It depends on what the user wants to accomplish. If only the probability of success in an English class is of interest, a scholastic aptitude test might well suffice—information concerning other abilities may not improve prediction enough to be worth obtaining. If several varied criteria are of interest, as in guidance into an academic, trade or commercial curriculum, the additional information provided by differential aptitude batteries should be well worth the effort. Interest in broad and varied criteria is greatest at the secondary school level, where the pupil reaches points of decision. At this time, the pupil and the school should be considering what kind of curriculum is best for him, what are appropriate directions and levels of aspiration for the immediate and the more distant future. Educational and vocational guidance are of tremendous importance; therefore, the broadest scope of ability testing is both desirable and eminently worthwhile. True, differential aptitude testing takes more time and costs more money. A two-, three-, or four-hour difference in time, or a dollar per pupil difference in cost, should be seen in the perspective of all the years of each student's educational and occupational future. The choices to be made may well set the pattern of the student's life; information to help guide those choices warrants the additional expenditure of minutes and pennies.

And in the Business World

The use of the educational frame of reference should not be taken to mean that the points do not apply to industry. They do. Readers engaged in personnel work in business and industry will have seen parallels between the last few paragraphs and their own problems, but will be conscious of some differences, too. For example, multi-score employment tests are often more useful than single-score tests in employee selection simply because they give a clearer picture of several aspects of ability that are mixed in unknown proportions in the single score. On the other hand, it is more often necessary for the industrial man than for the educator to make do with a less appropriate test. Many of the specific aptitude or achievement tests industry needs simply do not exist as yet, or do not work very well. In such cases, a general mental ability test or a semi-relevant aptitude test may be better than nothing even though we realize that a proficiency test would give us still more useful information about the applicant.

In Summary

Which kinds of tests are most helpful? Any test is helpful or harmful only as it is used properly or misused. The information which can be obtained from group tests of general intelligence, so-called, is often valuable. The information can be misinterpreted, and perhaps the use of the word "intelligence" predisposes somewhat to misinterpretation; but *any* test score can be misinterpreted. The issue is really whether scholastic aptitude or general mental ability tests provide *enough* information, and here one can only say "enough for what?" For some important decisions, and at some educational levels, the information is probably adequate. For other decisions, and at other levels, the additional information provided by differential ability tests is needed.

Whether achievement, intelligence or differential aptitude tests should be used depends on the functions to be served. The test user should ask "what inferences do I want to make; what information do I need to make those inferences?" The user who answers those questions will show intelligence, achievement of proficiency in test usage, and special aptitude for further advances in psychometrics.

13. Methods of Expressing Test Scores

Harold G. Seashore

An individual's test score acquires meaning when it can be compared with the scores of well-identified groups of people. Manuals for tests provide tables of norms to make it easy to compare individuals and groups. Several systems for deriving more meaningful "standard scores" from raw scores have been widely adopted. All of them reveal the relative status of individuals within a group.

The fundamental equivalence of the most popular standard score systems is illustrated in the chart (Figure 1). We hope the chart and the accompanying description will be useful to counselors, personnel officers, clinical diagnosticians, and others in helping them to show the uninitiated the essential simplicity of standard score systems, percentile equivalents, and their relation to the ideal normal distribution.

Sooner or later, every textbook discussion of test scores introduces the bell-shaped normal curve. The student of testing soon learns that many of the methods of deriving meaningful scores are anchored to the dimensions and characteristics of this curve, and he learns by observation of actual test score distributions that the ideal mathematical curve is a reasonably good approximation of many practical cases. He learns to use the standardized properties of the ideal curve as a model.

From *Test Service Bulletin,* Number 48, 1955, by Harold G. Seashore. Reprinted with consent of the Psychological Corporation, New York.

Let us look first at the curve itself. Notice that there are no raw scores printed along the baseline. The graph is generalized; it describes an idealized distribution of scores of any group on any test. We are free to use any numerical scale we like. For any particular set of scores, we can be arbitrary and call the average score zero. In technical terms we "equate" the mean raw score to zero. Similarly we can choose any convenient number, say 1.00, to represent the scale distance of one standard deviation.[1] Thus, if a distribution of scores on a particular test has a mean of 36 and a standard deviation of 4, the zero point on the baseline of our curve would be equivalent to an original score of 36; one unit to the right, $+1\sigma$, would be equivalent to 40, (36+4); and one unit to the left, -1σ, would be equivalent to 32, (36−4).

The total area under the curve represents the total number of scores in the distribution. Vertical lines have been drawn through the score scale (the baseline) at zero and at 1, 2, 3, and 4 sigma units to the right and left. These lines mark off subareas of the total area under the curve. The numbers printed in these subareas are per cents— *percentages of the total number of people.* Thus, 34.13 per cent of all cases in a normal distribution have scores falling between 0 and -1σ. For practical purposes we rarely need to deal with standard deviation units below −3 or above +3; the percentage of cases with scores beyond $\pm3\sigma$ is negligible.

The fact that 68.26 per cent fall between $\pm1\sigma$ gives rise to the common statement that in a normal distribution roughly two-thirds of all cases lie between plus and minus one sigma. This is a rule of thumb every test user should keep in mind. It is very near to the theoretical value and is a useful approximation.

Below the row of deviations expressed in sigma units is a row of per cents; these show *cumulatively* the percentage of people which is included *to the left* of each of the sigma points. Thus, starting from the left, when we reach the line erected above -2σ, we have

---

[1] The mathematical symbol for the standard deviation is the lower case Greek letter sigma or σ. These terms are used interchangeably in this article.

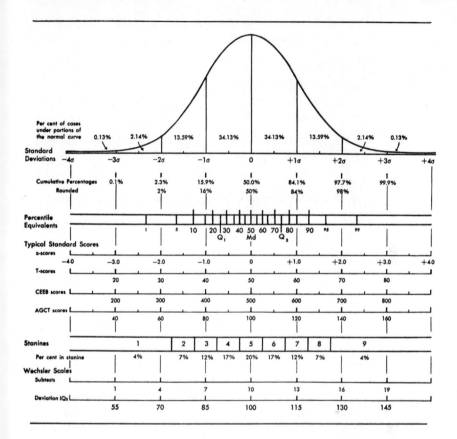

included the lowest 2.3 per cent of cases. These percentages have been rounded in the next row.

Note some other relationships: the area between the ±1σ points includes the scores which lie above the 16th percentile (−1σ) and below the 84th percentile (+1σ)—two major reference points all test users should know. When we find that an individual has a score 1σ above the mean, we conclude that his score ranks at the 84th percentile in the group of persons on whom the test was normed. (This conclusion is good provided we also add this clause, at least subvocally: *if this particular group reasonably approximates the ideal normal model.*)

The simplest facts to memorize about the normal distribution and the relation of the *percentile* system to deviations from the average in sigma units are seen in the chart. They are

Deviation from the mean	-2σ	-1σ	0	$+1\sigma$	$+2\sigma$
Percentile equivalent	2	16	50	84	98

To avoid cluttering the graph reference lines have not been drawn, but we could mark off ten per cent sections of area under the normal curve by drawing lines vertically from the indicated decile points (10, 20, . . . 80, 90) up through the graph. The reader might do this lightly with a colored pencil.

We can readily see that ten percent of the area (people) at the middle of the distribution embraces a smaller *distance* on the baseline of the curve than ten per cent of the area (people) at the ends of the range of scores, for the simple reason that the curve is much higher at the middle. A person who is at the 95th percentile is farther away from a person at the 85th percentile in units of *test score* than a person at the 55th percentile is from one at the 45th percentile.

The remainder of the chart, that is the several scoring scales drawn parallel to the baseline, illustrates variations of the *deviation score* principle. As a class these are called *standard scores*.

First, there are the *z-scores*. these are the same *numbers* as shown on the baseline of the graph; the only difference is that the expression, σ, has been omitted. These scores run, in practical terms, from -3.0 to $+3.0$. One can compute them to more decimal places if one wishes, although computing to a single place is usually sufficient. One can compute z-scores by equating the mean to 0.00 and the standard deviation to 1.00 for a distribution of any shape, but the relationships shown in this figure between the z-score equivalents of raw scores and percentile equivalents of raw scores are correct only for normal distributions. The interpretation of standard score systems derives from the idea of using the normal curve as a model.

As can be seen, T-scores are directly related to z-scores. The mean of the raw scores is equated to 50, and the standard deviation of the raw scores is equated to 10. Thus a z-score of +1.5 means the same as a T-score of 65. T-scores are usually expressed in whole numbers from about 20 to 80. The T-score plan eliminates negative numbers and thus facilitates many computations.[2]

The College Entrance Examination Board uses a plan in which both decimals and negative numbers are avoided by setting the arbitrary mean at 500 points and the arbitrary sigma at another convenient unit, namely, 100 points. The experienced tester or counselor who hears of a College Board SAT-V score of 550 at once thinks, "Half a sigma (50 points) above average (500 points) on the CEEB basic norms."

And when he hears of a score of 725 on SAT-N, he can interpret, "Plus 2¼σ. Therefore, better than the 98th percentile."

During World War II the Navy used the T-score plan of reporting test status. The Army used still another system with a mean of 100 and a standard deviation of 20 points.

Another derivative of the general standard score system is the *stanine* plan, developed by psychologists in the Air Force during the war. The plan divides the norm population into nine groups, hence, "standard nines." Except for stanine 9, the top, and stanine 1, the bottom, these groups are spaced in half-sigma units. Thus, stanine 5 is defined as including the people who are within ±0.25σ of the mean. Stanine 6 is the group defined by the half-sigma distance on the baseline between +0.25σ and +0.75σ. Stanines 1 and 9 include all persons who are below −1.75σ and above +1.75σ, respectively. The result is a distribution in which the mean is 5.0 and the standard deviation is 2.0.

Just below the line showing the demarcation of the nine groups in the stanine system there is a row of percentages which indicates the per cent of the total population in each of the stanines. Thus 7 per cent of

---

[2]T-scores and percentiles both have 50 as the main reference point, an occasional source of confusion to those who do not insist on careful labelling of data and of scores of individuals in their records.

the population will be in stanine 2, and 20 per cent in the middle group, stanine 5.

Interpretation of the Wechsler scales (W-B I, W-B II, WISC, and WAIS) depends on a knowledge of standard scores. A subject's raw score *on each of the subtests* in these scales is converted, by appropriate norms tables, to a standard score, based on a mean of 10 and a standard deviation of 3. The sums of standard scores on the Verbal Scale, the Performance Scale, and the Full Scale are then converted into IQs. These IQs are based on a standard score mean of 100, the conventional number for representing the IQ of the average person in a given age group. The standard deviation of the IQs is set at 15 points. In practical terms, then, roughly two-thirds of the IQs are between 85 and 115, that is, $\pm 1\sigma$[3]. IQs of the type used in the Wechsler scales have come to be known as *deviation IQs,* as contrasted with the IQs developed from scales in which a derived mental age is divided by chronological age.

Users of the Wechsler scales should establish clearly in their minds the relationship of subtest scaled scores and the deviation IQs to the other standard score systems, to the ordinary percentile rank interpretation, and to the deviation units on the baseline of the normal curve. For example, every Wechsler examiner should recognize that an IQ of 130 is a score equivalent to a deviation of $+2\sigma$, and that this IQ score delimits approximately the upper two per cent of the population. If a clinician wants to evaluate a Wechsler IQ of 85 along with percentile ranks on several other tests given in school, he can mentally convert the IQ of 85 to a percentile rank of about 16, this being the percentile equal to a deviation from the mean of -1σ. Of course he should also consider the appropriateness and comparability of norms.

---

[3] Every once in a while we receive a letter from someone who suggests that the Wechsler scales ought to generate a wider range of IQs. The reply is very simple. If we want a wider range of IQs all we have to do is choose a *larger arbitrary* standard deviation, say, 20 or 25. Under the present system, $\pm 3\sigma$ gives IQs of 55 to 145, with a few rare cases below and a few rare cases above. If we used 20 as the standard deviation, we would *arbitrarily* increase the $\pm 3\sigma$ range of IQs from 55–145 to 40–160. This is a wider range of numbers! But, test users should never forget that adaptions of this kind do not change the responses of the people who took the test, do not change the order of the persons in relation to each other, and do not change the psychological meaning attached to an IQ.

Efficiency in interpreting test scores in counseling, in clinical diagnosis, and in personnel selection depends, in part, on facility in thinking in terms of the major interrelated plans by which meaningful scores are derived from raw scores. It is hoped that this graphic presentation will be helpful to all who in their daily work must help others understand the information conveyed by numerical test scores.

14. Myths About Intelligence

Roger Reger

School psychologists are faced with a continuously growing body of folklore about intelligence and intelligence tests. This problem is not endemic to school psychology, but school psychologists are in the unique position of being the most vulnerable to this folklore and at the same time in a position to begin culling myth from fact.

The over-all problem presented by this folklore will not be an easy one to resolve. Much of the folklore is so steeped in tradition that its very longevity can be used as an emotionally-laden argument for its fancied verity. Similarly, the widespread—even universal—acceptance of these fictions as fact makes their recognition most difficult.

"Basic" Myths

Probably the most effective preservative of myths about intelligence and intelligence tests are the pseudo-arguments that purport to challenge certain of these myths, when in fact they result in a strengthening of the over-all illusion.

MYTH #1: RELIABILITY AS VALIDITY

One of these pseudo-arguments is presented in the form of questions about the *validity* of intelligence tests

From *Psychology in the Schools,* 1966, *3:* 39–44. Reprinted with permission of Roger Reger and *Psychology in the Schools,* Psychology Press, Inc.

(e.g., "How do we know that an intelligence test measures what it is supposed to measure?"). These questions invariably are appropriate and in need of investigation. But just as invariably the questions are answered in terms of *reliability* rather than validity (Cattell, 1964).

At a less sophisticated level, questions related to such matters as "the constancy of the IQ," more obviously matters of reliability, sometimes are discussed as if validity were the issue being considered. As Cureton (1950) suggests, using a measure to predict itself is hardly a test of validity.

Hagen (1963) notes that in spite of existing weaknesses, intelligence tests are the best available predictors of academic success. However, she then illustrates the weaknesses of intelligence tests by comparing them with the unreliability of bathroom scales and dressmakers' measurements. Neel (1964) similarly presents questions relating to validity and then discusses these questions in terms of reliability.

Intelligence tests today are, in fact, tacitly assumed to be self-validating (though sometimes unreliable!). Scores from a test that measures intelligence are assumed to be as self-evident (i.e., valid) as "scores" obtained from a yardstick that measures height. A child is placed at a "level" of intellectual ability that allows a comparison to be made with his age peers, just as he is placed at a "level" of height that allows similar age-peer comparisons. Nevertheless, this analogy is inappropriate. Yardsticks (and bathroom scales) are direct measures. Intelligence tests, on the other hand, do not directly measure "intelligence," but *infer* that intelligence is somehow indirectly being measured (Benton, 1964; Rawlings, 1963, p.361).

Validity remains an essential but largely ignored feature of intelligence tests. Confusing reliability with validity is a fertile source of folklore.

MYTH #2: DESCRIPTION AS EXPLANATION

Gallagher (1964) states that "Intelligence tests have served in three rather distinct capacities: (a) prediction, (b) classification, and (c) diagnosis" (p.499). Gallagher and Moss (1963) earlier had discussed this in more detail. However, it seems that ultimately classification and diagnosis are based on predictions. As Thorndike (1964) observes, "Decisions imply predictions" (p. 104). In this intricate area lies the source of another rich spring of folklore.

Mythology abounds from failure to recognize that intelligence tests are predictive devices, and nothing more. Astin (1964) states that "In developing a test which is to be used primarily in an applied setting, investigators frequently construct, 'standardize,' and market the test first, and look around for criteria against which to 'validate' it afterward. It is an understatement to say that this practice is an anachronism" (p. 814).

The contents of intelligence tests are necessarily derived from the core of social and cultural knowledge, and it is this same core from which the school curriculum is derived. Thus, in a very significant sense, intelligence tests measure school-related knowledge. Indeed, Hagen (1963) acknowledges that "many people feel that 'general intelligence' is a misnomer for this test—that 'scholastic aptitude' would be a more precise term" (p. 6).

It is understandable that minority and/or "culturally deprived" groups typically score low on intelligence tests (Kennedy, Van de Riet, & White, 1963; Neel, 1964). In this case it is irrelevant to focus on the tests as being "unfair," because the *predictions* that can be derived from the tests are only reflecting an actual condition and are in themselves justifiable (McNemar, 1964). Intelligence tests are unfair only when they are inappropriately used for direct classification and diagnosis. It is unfair, at any time, to deny any school age child educational opportunities because he happens to score low on an intelligence test.

Consider the low-performing child referred to a school psychologist. It is found that the child scores low on a measure of school-related knowledge. This legitimately allows the school psychologist to state the prediction that the child's performance in school will be poor for some *unknown* length of time. It is of questionable appropriateness for the school psychologist to state that the low-scoring child is mentally retarded, and that his mental retardation in turn *explains* why he probably will have difficulty with school work (Staats & Staats, 1963). The thinking in that case becomes circular: a child's performance is poor; therefore, he is mentally retarded; therefore, his mental retardation explains his poor performance. Description is used as if explanation and prediction were being invoked[1] (Ellis, 1963).

"Secondary" Myths

Following are capsule outlines of other myths, some of which derive from the two major sources suggested so far: confusion between validity and reliability, and circular descriptive thinking used as explanation and prediction.

MYTH #3: THE IQ AS A BODILY ORGAN

A child does not "have" an IQ; an IQ is only a measuring device. The assumption that the test measures something inside the child (his IQ) is frankly ridiculous. However, belief that the IQ is a real internal characteristic is fairly common. Even such an illustrious figure as E. A. Doll (1964), in discussing the relative merits of mental age versus IQ, has made the curious statement that "we learn with our mental ages rather than our IQ's" (p. 39).

Because children do not possess a mysterious internal organ called "a real IQ," it is useless to pursue this phantom with relentless testing, as it will invariably escape.

MYTH #4: IQ FUNCTIONING

The idea of "depressed" intelligence, sometimes leading to the anomalous "diagnosis" of pseudofeeble-mindedness (Arthur, 1947; Cantor, 1955), is depressing. Such an idea carries the assumption that there is such a

---

[1]There are educational implications involved in thinking, not of "mental" retardation, but of predicted *educational retardation*. See "The Concept of Educational Handicap" in Reger (1965), and "Special Education and the Concept of Educational Handicap." Reger (Unpublished manuscript).

thing as "a real IQ," or a static but "covered" level of intelligence (perhaps covered with a pseudogeological "emotional overlay").

According to such an assumption it follows that intelligence tests often fail to ferret out this real IQ, and *only* for this reason are often said to be "inaccurate." Therefore, it is asserted that a determination from "other factors" must help in the diagnosis of mental retardation, a subjective process which sometimes is suggested as being outside the competence of test-bound psychologists (Hirning, 1964).

MYTH #5: PREDICTING versus DETERMINING PERFORMANCE

Such phrases as "working up to the IQ," or "the functioning IQ level," contain the explicit assumption that not only should intelligence test performance *predict* school performance, it should *determine* school performance. This myth is the source of the "over-achievement" notion. Carter (1964), for example, states that "over- and under-achievers are those who achieve more, or less, respectively, than expected in the light of measured intelligence" (p. 175).

The determination of performance undoubtedly has an interaction effect on predictions. Babbott and Grant (1964), and Edwards and Kirby (1964), for example, studied the usefulness of IQ scores in "predicting" academic success. They computed correlations between IQ scores and grades or achievement scores in several areas, using data obtained from records of past events. These typical studies leave unanswered the question of whether or not IQ scores in fact partially determined the grades or achievement expectations presented to the students by the teachers.

MYTH #6: RAISING THE POPULATION IQ

Because intelligence tests are statistical artifacts (Gerberich, 1963), it is meaningless to talk about "increases in IQ" in the population at large. If a test is standardized with a certain mean and standard deviation, and subsequent surveys show that the population actually has a "higher IQ" than the putative mean, this would suggest faulty test construction more than anything else.

The idea that the intelligence of children increases with age, in the sense that individual children who score 105 at one age might score 115 at a later age, which now and then is suggested, is another impossibility simply because of the way in which intelligence tests are statistically designed. This is true not only for recently devised tests, but also for older tests, such as the 1937 Stanford-Binet. If it were found, for example, that children knew "twice as much" at age ten as they did at age eight, individual children who scored 100 on a test at age eight would still score 100 at age ten because, even though they have become "smarter," so have their peers with whom they are being compared.

Many feel that the use of "mental age" on older tests gets around this problem but they have only concretized the mental age *concept* and assume that it, too, like the IQ, is a characteristic of children rather than of measuring devices. Again, children do not "have" a mental age any more than they "have" an IQ. If there are changes in the mental age scores of same-age groups of children over the years it is extremely difficult to determine the reasons for these changes. It is possible, for example, that many of the items in the 1937 Stanford-Binet have been incorporated into the school curriculum of today. While this should be reflected currently in higher scores than we obtained 15 years ago, particularly among younger and brighter children (as found, in fact, by Lindholm, 1964), it is pointless to assert that this is a reflection of a higher general level of population intelligence.

MYTH #7: LOW PERFORMANCE AS SUBHUMAN

Finally, the terms used to refer to low-performing children are sad reflections on the sophistication of the professions.

Consider the following sordid collection of terms: weakminded, feeble-minded, backward, or stupid children; morons, imbeciles, idiots, simpletons, dolts, oafs, blockheads, ignoramuses, vegetables, Mongoloids (and other type-labels), retards, retardates, garden variety retardates, high or low grade retardates, defectives, familials, aments, organics, good organics, dummies, dumbbells, dullards, dodos, subnormals "a sixty-five" (or some other number), untrainables, trainables, TMRs or TMHs, and educables, EMRs, or EMHs.

Most of these are terms of invective, of scorn and disdain. Admittedly, changing words does not necessarily take away an existing stigma. If a group carries a stigma, it will not be long before new words applied to the group (e.g., exceptional, slow learning) take on the aroma of the stigma. But referring to children as if they were livestock or vegetation, or simply numbers, certainly does not help matters.

More importantly, the condescending paternalism with which low-performing children are treated today hardly suggests that sincere efforts are being made to ease the stigma itself. From an educational standpoint, is there really something "wrong" with low-performing children or rather is there more often something wrong with the educational conditions (including attitudes) provided for such children?

Conclusions

The following conclusions are drawn from this brief examination of folklore about intelligence and intelligence tests:

First, the only legitimate use of intelligence tests is for predictive purposes. Other purported uses depend upon prediction.

Second, it is not justifiable for educational personnel to say that a child is mentally retarded on the basis of results from an intelligence test or from observations of classroom performance. It *is* justifiable to state that a prediction can be made about educational performance on the basis of results from intelligence tests. Thus, educational retardation can be predicted from low performance on intelligence tests.

"Mental retardation" is a noneducationally-relevant conception of a behavioral condition that produces no significant consequences for educational programing;

educational retardation, on the other hand, is highly relevant to educational programing with important consequences.

Third, if sense is not substituted for nonsense in the use of intelligence tests, it will become more and more apparent that their use in the schools should be curtailed or eliminated entirely. Continued gross misuse of tests and ignorance about the meaning of test results is leading in this direction.

McNemar (1964) reasonably suggests that "it is high time for the profession to establish a bureau of standards to test the tests instead of coasting down a road that is tinged with some of the trappings of Madison Avenue. Better to have informed control than ignorant, hostile, external control" (p. 876). Even so, control of test construction and distribution will not control the inappropriate use of tests. There are good tests available today but their misuse often makes them worthless.

Fourth, it is time to begin eliminating the prejudice that exists about low-performing children. Educationally retarded children in the schools do not need "help" (i.e., condescending "understanding" and pity); they need educational opportunities. Teachers who work with educationally retarded children are engaging in challenging work for which they should receive adequate pay and professional satisfactions.

REFERENCES

Arthur, G. Pseudo-feeblemindedness. *American Journal of Mental Deficiency*, 1947, 52, 147-142.

Astin, A. W. Criterion-centered research. *Educational and Psychological Measurements*, 1964, 24, 807-822.

Babbott, E. F., and Grant, C. W. I.Q. as one of several variables in predicting academic success. *The School Counselor*, 1964, 12, 18-21.

Benton, A. L. Psychological evaluation and differential diagnosis. In H. A. Stevens, and R. Heber (Eds.), *Mental retardation*. Chicago: Univer. of Chicago Press, 1964. Pp. 16-56.

Cantor, G. N. On the incurability of mental deficiency. *American Journal of Mental Deficiency*, 1955, 60, 362-265.

Carter, H. D. Over- and under-achievement in reading. *California Journal of Educational Research*, 1964,15,175-183.

Cattell, R. B. Validity and reliability; a proposed more basic set of concepts. *Journal of Educational Psychology*, 1964, 55, 1-22.

Cureton, E. E. Validity, reliability and baloney. *Educational and Psychological Measurement*, 1950, 10, 94-96.

Doll, E. A. Mental age versus IQ. *The Pointer*, 1964, 8 (3), 339-40.

Edwards, A. J., and Kirby, M. Elsie. Predictive efficiency of intelligence test scores: intelligence quotients obtained in grade one and achievement test scores obtained in grade three. *Educational and Psychological Measurement*, 1964, 24, 941-946.

Ellis, N. R. (Ed.) Introduction. *Handbook of Mental Deficiency*. New York: McGraw-Hill, 1963. Pp. 1-7.

Gallagher, J. J. Meaningful learning and retention: intrapersonal cognitive variables. *Review of Educational Research*, 1964, 34, 499-512.

Gallagher, J. J., and Moss, J. W. New concepts of intelligence and their effect on exceptional children. *Exceptional Childern*, 1963, 30, 1-5.

Gerberich, J. R. The development of educational testing. *Theory into Practice*, 1963, 2, 184-191.

Hagen, Elizabeth. Standardized tests: tyranny or tools? *Teaching and Learning*, 1963. 5-11.

Hirning, L. C. Some experiences in school psychiatry. *Teachers College Record*, 1964, 66,64-70.

Kennedy, W. A., Van de Riet, V., and White, J. C., Jr. A normative sample of intelligence and achievement of Negro elementary school children in the Southeastern United States. *Monographs of the Society for Research in Child Development*, 1963, Series No. 90, 28, No. 6.

Lindholm, B. W. Changes in conventional and deviation IQ's. *Journal of Educational Psychology*, 1964, 55, 110-113.

McNemar, Q. Lost, our intelligence? Why? *American Psychologist*, 1964, 19, 871-882.

Neel, Ann F. What does IQ mean? *Clinical Pediatrics*, 1964, 3, 374-378.

Rawlings, Grace. Examination and diagnosis. In R. F. Tredgold, and K. Soddy (Eds.), *Textbook of mental deficiency (subnormality)*. Baltimore: Willians & Wilkins, 1963. Pp. 357-409.

Reger, R. *School psychology*. Springfield, Ill.: Charles C. Thomas, 1965.

Reger, R. Special education and the concept of educational handicap. Unpublished manuscript.

Staats, A. W., and Staats, Carolyn K. *Complex human behavior: a systematic extension of learning principles*. New York: Holt, Rinehart & Winston, 1963.

Thorndike, R. L. Educational decisions and human assessment. *Teachers College Record*, 1964, 66, 103-112.

15. Factors that Affect Test Results

Warren G. Findley

We talk quite freely of "giving" and "taking" tests. But "giving tests" is a more complex activity than that short phrase implies and we are warranted in using the more pretentious phrase, "administration of a testing program." Similarly, we need to turn from the simple view implied in the phrase "taking tests" to what might be called "acceptance of testing" on the part of those examined.

What do we mean by acceptance of testing? Early in World War II, the late Walter V. Bingham was discussing the new Army General Classification Test developed under his direction. This was a general aptitude measure and included vocabulary, arithmetic, and spatial relations items. The latter items had been drawn from a college entrance test and consisted of views of piles of "blocks" that were equal in size. The examinee was asked to tell how many such blocks there must be in each pile to support the ones showing. "Why, oh, why," complained Dr. Bingham, "didn't we call them 'boxes' instead of 'blocks'?" His GI examinees readily accepted the vocabulary and arithmetic items as fair game, relevant to evaluating their general usefulness in many activities. In Dr. Bingham's view, they would have accepted as equally relevant the task of counting "boxes," such as they might have seen on any loading

From *National Elementary Principal,* 1961, *41:* 6–10. Copyright 1961 by the Department of Elementary School Principals, National Education Association. All rights reserved. Reprinted with permission of the author and publisher.

platform, but "blocks" were what their little brothers and sisters played with, hardly a man's fare. This fine point in acceptance had been missed in designing the test. It had not been a factor when the blocks were used in college testing because the examinees were accustomed to testing of many varieties and tended to come from scholastic and social circles in which puzzles, if not parlor games, were readily accepted as fair challenges to employ one's wits.

This author retains a vivid memory of his experience in coping with the fury of two WAC sergeants who were taking an extension course in psychology and had been given a psychological examination. These bright young women, who did well in the course generally, spent a good 30 minutes berating their instructor over the figure analogies test in the battery. It involved seeing relations among abstract figures. To them, this appeared a trivial, totally unfair exercise in dealing with wiggly lines that had no meaning. They did not accept the test and could hardly have done themselves full justice on it. Others have reported that women reject such testing more than men do. The sex difference in achievement on such tests is substantial and may be accounted for, at least partially, by the lack of acceptance among women of these tests.

One step closer to the elementary school is the doctoral study by Machover in which he found that delinquent boys fell farthest below the norms of their nondeviant contemporaries on test of spatial relations and nonverbal reasoning of the sort described in the two previous illustrations. They had been given these tests in an effort to appraise their mental ability, free of the influence of the cultural and educational factors involved in tests of reading, vocabulary, and arithmetic. What seem to be even more deeply ingrained by cultural experience are attitudes toward intrinsically "meaningless" or irrelevant abstract exercises. The more hopeful type of nonverbal test appears to be one based on pictures. Pictures are meaningful and are accepted as such.

Let us now consider the factors affecting test results in terms of the pupil, the teacher, the immediate situation, and the broader situation in which the testing takes place.

THE PUPIL AND TESTING

How does the pupil approach testing? It is certainly not true that each child sits eager-eyed waiting for his teacher to give him the opportunity to show what he can do on a test, proceeds immediately and efficiently with each task set before him, and puts his best foot forward on each and every occasion. Many factors affect his acceptance of testing.

For one thing, his age and maturity affect the period over which the pupil may be expected to give full attention. Standardized tests take attention span into account. The teacher is well advised to give a test at more than one sitting if the test directions permit. Unless the class is obviously more mature than most, it is best to use the maximum number of sittings proposed.

Particularly at early ages, many children are easily distracted. A bird flying past the window, the backfire of a passing truck, the dropping of a pencil will distract many a child and prevent his doing himself justice. Someone entering the testing room or—perish the thought—a schoolwide announcement over the P.A. system is particularly serious. Most test publishers offer signs to hang on the doors of rooms where testing is in progress. It is also essential to follow directions specifying that testing is to be done in groups of a certain size in order to control distraction and assure that pupils master instructions before they begin.

The factors of limited attention span and distractibility make it virtually impossible to be sure that primary grade children have shown their real ability on a group test of mental ability. This is true of all group testing at this level. It is a less serious consideration in testing readiness or reading progress because these measures have a limited objective of predicting success in immediate learning and are only part of the evidence used by the teacher in planning instruction. It is more serious with group tests of mental ability, with their inevitable

IQ's, because they imply prediction over a longer range of time and undependability of individual performance can have pernicious effects.

An individual test, on the other hand, allows the skilled examiner to so adapt the test and the testing situation to the individual child that we can insure his acceptance of the test as fair, appropriate, even enjoyable, or note rather confidently that such acceptance did not prevail and that the test interpretation must be qualified. In group testing, our goal can only be to establish the best conditions for group work, with only that attention to individuals which is possible in a classroom group, and then trust that an individual child's acceptance of the test reflects his learning capacity and/or working knowledge in a classroom group.

Test directions are crucial. The examinee must understand what he is to do and we must impose no unnecessary hazards. Tests for young children commonly provide for reading aloud the directions, if not the questions themselves. One may *not,* of course, read a standardized test aloud unless the instructions so specify, but this restriction happily does not apply to classroom testing. In testing third-graders who have been taking a science course organized about an educational television program, we regularly instruct teachers to read the questions and alternative answers aloud *twice* before the pupils underline the correct answer. We must use words children understand but cannot read independently if we are to test important outcomes. Teachers rapidly learn to avoid pauses, inflections, or involuntary facial expressions that reveal the correct answer.

Reading looms as so large a factor in many standardized tests that the question arises of whether each part is just another test of reading rather than of the skill or knowledge area designated in the title. Because they make such a heavy demand on reading, many school systems do not use standardized achievement tests below the third or fourth grade, except in reading.

At higher grade levels, reading continues to present a problem in evaluation of achievement. We often say that reading is essential in arithmetic because the pupil must be able to read and interpret "word" problems. We forget it is we who create written textbooks, write problems on the board, and give standardized tests with written problems, whereas many of life's problems spring from concrete materials, oral questions, or numerical data as such.

Much can be done by the alert teacher to reduce the reading complication in classroom testing, but even standardized testing can be adapted to pupils' reading levels. Achievement test batteries come at several levels—primary, elementary, intermediate, advanced—and can be given to children in groups at their reading level. One of the newer series has attacked this problem directly by offering tests at all levels with the same instructions, same number of questions, and same time limits. Tests at different levels in this series can thus be given by the teachers in the regular classes. But any test battery can be used similarly if the children are grouped by reading level. Some may question the comparability of scores obtained by such adaptations, but it is certainly true in the individual case that more useful information can be obtained by testing at a child's reading level than by letting him fall down on a test he can hardly read. For that matter, a case can be made for the fact that a child may obtain a meaninglessly high score by chance marking on a test above his level simply because the score scale for the advanced test does not extend down to the individual's true level.

The problem of cheating on tests arises here. Although it has always been with us, cheating presents a new face now that we encourage group work on many projects. We owe it to our children to clarify this distinction between working together for group purposes and working separately for individual mastery. So far as possible, we should make it easy to work singly and difficult to "copy" when we want individual mastery. Adapting testing to a level commensurate with a pupil's competence will simplify his learning the habit of working for himself.

THE TEACHER AND TESTING

Through all these discussions of testing runs a thread of insistence that testing must have as a central purpose helping teachers help children to learn. The teacher must perceive testing in this framework if he is to convey its purpose to the pupils and if the testing program is thereby to become an integral part of the instructional program, accepted by teachers and pupils alike. No matter how carefully other desirable practices in the use of tests are followed, they will fail in their effectiveness if testing is not seen as a means of helping the teacher do better what he must do anyway—teach. This sense of purpose and usefulness in testing does not require an elaborate build-up, but it does require some preparation of pupils by a simple statement at their level of understanding, preferably the day before the test. Use of test results to help the pupil help himself in grade after grade will make the acceptance of testing a matter of habitual good morale.

The administrator, too, must accept testing as an aid to teaching. Many of us argue that this intention is most clearly conveyed by annual fall testing of achievement, which provides up-to-date information about a class when the pupils are new to the teacher. No evaluation of the teaching can be inferred in testing at this point. Additional testing at other times may be optional or, if uniform, may be justified to obtain helpful information before instruction begins in a specific area.

The teacher's use of classroom tests needs to have this same purpose of helping to learn. Highly competitive grading procedures and constant praise of outstanding achievers (usually the same ones) need to give way to more individualized approaches. Testing at the end of a unit thus becomes a means of ascertaining what group and individual reteaching is needed, as well as ascertaining what has been learned. Cheating then loses its motive.

This morale factor becomes particularly important in appraising personal-social factors. Habitual use of tests and other evaluation devices to help pupils help themselves is the best assurance that the twin sources of undependability—distortion and indifference—can be controlled. It is obvious that measures of interest, personality, attitudes, or sociometric choice can be answered in such a way as to present a false picture of one's feelings which may serve the purpose of winning approval by the teacher. Where there are no right answers in the sense that achievement tests require, but only matters of choice, the pupil may give answers he thinks are "wanted." If he is used to having results used confidentially and helpfully, he will respond in a normal way, neither presenting calculated answers nor irresponsibly marking meaningless choices.

A corollary of the use of tests to help pupils help themselves is a voluntary limitation on the number of tests used, so that pupils do not get the feeling of being overtested "guinea pigs." Each school administrator and teacher must be the judge of when a feeling of overtesting is in prospect. Purposefulness in all testing is the best controlling factor, but the climate of acceptance needs to be watched since loss of acceptance of testing is a matter of serious concern and may prove very difficult to correct.

A word about the tasks of giving and scoring tests and recording the results. Acceptance of testing for it helpfulness by teachers and pupils is the basic guarantee of dependable results, but a sense of concern for precision needs to be developed. Failure to maintain testing conditions specified in a test manual can destroy the usefulness of the results. No help may be given students beyond that specified, nor may time limits be disregarded if virtually all or none of the pupils seem to have finished. Test publishers go to great lengths to make directions so clear that no further help is required after work begins. They are equally careful to set time limits so the great majority of appropriate examinees will finish each test or reach the limit of their ability before time is called. If the test appears too difficult (long) or too easy, it is better to consider giving a more elementary or more advanced test.

Scoring is a chore, no doubt of it. But incorrect scores are serious if they are given any weight in determining immediate assignments or instruction, and even more serious if they are used as "cold facts" some time later. In most schools, it is desirable to use hand-scored tests to avoid the pupils' having to cross-reference between test questions and answer spaces. Local studies may reveal that separate answer sheets can be used as early as fourth grade with no disadvantage, but this will not be true generally. It is best to accept hand-scoring as a chore necessary to afford pupils the best chance to show their true competence, and then organize for efficient, cheerful scoring.

Recording test results requires clerical precision and checking. It may be delegated, but there is much to be said for the interested party, the teacher, attending to this, too. Class record sheets that come with published tests or local adaptions can reduce the chore to a minimum. Plotting individual scores on pupil profiles should reveal strengths and weaknesses that might be over-looked. In keeping with the concept of helping pupils help themselves, pupils may be enlisted to draw their own profiles and thus understand better the progress they are making.

THE TEST SITUATION

We have mentioned the need for advance notice of testing and a general atmosphere of understood purpose to produce an acceptance of testing. Good lighting, reasonable comfort and work space, and uninterrupted working time are also essential. A few other points may be made.

Early in the history of standardized testing, there was considerable concern over the effect on tested achievement of such factors as health, emotion, and even time of day. There seems to be only a minimum of significant observations to pass on. The only time of day to be avoided is after eating a heavy lunch or after vigorous exercise. There appears to be no evidence to support the idea that the best time is at the start of the day "when everyone's fresh." A little better is after everyone is "in the groove"—anytime a normal atmosphere of study purpose had developed.

"Not feeling well" is generally unimportant, not because poor physical condition is unimportant, but because reported poor immediate health requires verification of cause. We all have some anxiety about taking a test, as we do about speaking in public. It is now generally accepted that it is natural and even desirable to feel some concern about a public talk; lack of it may indicate inadequate preparation. In the same way, studies by Sarason and others show that moderate test anxiety is characteristic of our best achievers and is to be expected in all. Serious anxiety distracts, and it increases as a test is perceived to be more difficult. This argues again for setting each pupil the standardized test that fits his level of competence. Anxiety that overruns normal symptoms of uneasiness calls for case study to reach and cope with the basic causes.

It should hardly be necessary to advise against testing when exciting events are in prospect. Holding children overtime at lunch or the end of the day, or testing the day school closes for a holiday, the day of an important game or early dismissal to visit the zoo, or on occasions marked by news of a tragic event will generally affect so many pupils' test performance adversely that testing is inadvisable. Similar circumstances affecting an individual would warrant rescheduling his test.

THE BROADER SOCIAL BACKGROUND

Factors of socio-economic status, school expenditure, school size, ethnic group, section of country, and urban-rural status have been found to be associated with test performance in elementary schools. The underlying factors are often hard to find. The perennial question of the relative importance of heredity and environment virtually defies solution. Favorable heredity and environment tend to go together, as do unfavorable heredity and environments. Individuals are found in all environments who attain great heights; some from even the most favored areas wind up in lives of crime and dissipation. What useful generalizations are available?

Socio-economic status of the patrons of a school is probably the most central factor. School expenditures are dependent on it in many communities and the other factors are at least complicated by its operation. What is generally found associated with socio-economic status is an attitude toward schools and schooling which affects not merely financial support of schools, but also the quality of English spoken in the home and the neighborhood; the attention given to learning to read, including the provision of reading matter in the home; the emphasis on study and provision for both time and place for study; stability of home arrangements; the respect accorded learning and learned persons; and the expectation of higher education.

The basic community attitudes that affect achievement should be dealt with directly. Children from underprivileged neighborhoods will tend to be even more retarded educationally than they are mentally, but this does not suggest allowing for such retardation. Rather, the challenge is, through every promotional program possible and special educational opportunities, to interest the parents in helping their children as they have never done before. Relating present to past achievement sets goals of modest improvement that can be steadily sought. The same approach can save the favored areas from settled smugness or feverish effort and pressure based on impractical, perfectionistic goals.

Ethnic differences often provoke fruitless argument and unprofitable speculation. The concomitants of socio-economic status that were enumerated are generally associated with ethnic differences on achievement and mental ability tests. The ethnic differences are real on the average, but individual excellence in generally depressed ethnic groups is usually explicable in terms of special circumstances. Statistical data might suggest that a correction should be made to aptitude scores of children from underprivileged groups to take account of disadvantages they suffer. The adjustment, however, would overcorrect for those in the underprivileged ethnic group who did not suffer the disadvantages commonly associated with their group, while leaving uncorrected the score of the individual from the generally favored ethnic group who was himself underprivileged.

Put another way, the variations in achievement *within* ethnic groups are far greater than the average differences *between* the groups. In discussing Negro-white differences, a Negro professor made his point dramatically by saying that at his college they were not interested in whether a student could do "culture-fair" arithmetic but rather in whether he could do arithmetic.

Findings of regional differences in general achievement are based to a considerable extent on differences in proportions of urban and rural pupils. Urban pupils do better. They have larger schools offering better instruction by better paid teachers. Again, neither regional norms nor separate norms for urban and rural schools are to be recommended. Regional norms simply favor the cities in largely rural areas and discriminate against rural children in heavily urban areas.

Local norms based on current achievement, with improvement over past performance as the goal, are recommended. The individual may well be compared with his immediate peers, as well as with a still hypothetical national norm group.

To return to our concept of acceptance of testing, it is fair to say that urban and suburban children and those from favored socio-economic neighborhoods accept testing more readily than do rural or underprivileged children. Tests are a part of their culture, are respected by their parents as useful objective supplements to teacher judgment based on recitations and other noncomparable evidence from special projects and work products. Tests are like the parlor games that are played in their circle at social gatherings. However, standardized tests are becoming a well-established feature of all schooling and we may fairly hope they reflect goals increasingly accepted by all sectors of the school population. Testing used to help teachers help children help themselves is the keystone.

16. Assessing the Intelligence of Disadvantaged Children

Joseph Justman

In any urban school system, one can identify a large group of pupils, characterized by low motivation and lack of goals, whose school performance is substandard. Predominantly, such children are drawn from homes where the adults have had little schooling. In many instances, large family size, poverty, discrimination, high mobility, and slum conditions are complicating factors. Typically, the child from such homes is disadvantaged—he enters school lacking the experiences, skills, and values of his nondisadvantaged peer.

Much more important than defining exactly what is meant by the term "disadvantaged children" is noting the extent to which they are found in the classroom. Truly, the number and proportion of such children in our large urban areas is staggering. According to one estimate, by 1970 one of every two pupils in the public schools of the 15 largest cities in the United States will be drawn from our so-called culturally disadvantaged or socially deprived groups. Granted that there may be considerable error in this projection; the exact data are not too important. Even if the stated number and proportion of such children in urban schools does represent an over-estimate, it is abundantly clear that dealing with disadvantaged children is one of the most pressing educational problems facing school people at the present time.

Reprinted from the February, 1967, issue of *Education*. Copyright © 1967 by the Bobbs-Merrill Co., Inc., Indianapolis, Indiana. Reprinted with consent of author and publisher.

Schools in the United States are committed to the principle of providing to all children the means of attaining a modicum of success in our society. But "success" is becoming more and more difficult to achieve without some degree of specialized training. The pattern of occupations in the United States is changing very rapidly, and the proportion of available jobs that do not require specialized education and training is diminishing at an increasing rate. The individual who presents himself to an employer without a marketable skill finds himself relegated to the waste heap. It is the disadvantaged child who most often fails to attain the minimum requirements needed for success for the present-day world of work, who becomes the cast-off, the discard, the frustrated. To the extent that potential job-seekers are not provided with those skills that will enable them to compete for a share in the benefits of our society, we foster, as Dr. Conant warns, "social dynamite."

There is another aspect of the problem that merits consideration. Our society is rapidly approaching a crisis in the development of technicians and professional workers in almost every field. We simply do not have enough doctors, physicists, teachers, or engineers, nor do we have enough technically trained workers to meet the needs in our increasingly automated industries.

At the present time, such professional and technical personnel are drawn from the upper third, or perhaps, the top half of our student population. But this proportion of our students does not provide the number of persons we need to fill current and projected demands for professionals and technicians. To provide such workers, we must seek to discover potential personnel in the untapped human resources of disadvantaged children that now constitute perhaps one-third of the population of our schools. We must locate, among the large numbers of disadvantaged children, those who are capable of meeting society's demands for high level skills.

Whatever our motivation—whether we think in broad terms of providing full self-realization for every child, or in the narrower sense of filling our needs for talented individuals—our concern must be directed to assessing the potential of the disadvantaged child. The most useful tools that we have at our disposal in this task of appraisal are educational and psychological tests. Such test are powerful tools, but their intelligent use calls for special training. No responsible civic authority would permit an individual to operate an X-ray machine who was untrained in its use or who was unaware of the damage it could cause if improperly used. Responsible educational authorities realize that it is just as foolhardy to permit untrained personnel to administer tests. Caution in test administration and in test interpretation is even more important when one seeks to use tests with disadvantaged children.

What, then, are some of the problems that one encounters in using tests with disadvantaged groups?

THE PROBLEM OF BIAS

What is meant by "bias"? In general, bias refers to the influence of factors not relevant to the purpose of measurement on test scores. The degree of bias and purity of measure, what is usually referred to as test validity, are inversely related—as bias goes up, validity goes down.

What is involved in building an unbiased test? In the early stages of his work, Binet noted that intelligence tests must be free from the influence of knowledges and skills ordinarily associated with school training, and endeavored to eliminate such culturally biased tasks from his test materials, in an attempt to develop a test that was not contaminated by experiential influences.

Thorndike and his coworkers expressed much the same point of view in the late 1920's. Defining intelligence as the ability to learn, they felt that the more intelligent person should "be able to learn harder things, or to be able to learn the same thing more quickly." In constructing intelligence tests, therefore, the best procedure would be to equalize environmental forces by (1) using a wide variety of tasks with which all persons have had adequate experience; (2) using novel tasks to which no individual will have been previously exposed; and (3) using tasks that are so familiar that everyone has had adequate environmental stimulation to master them.

In the more recent past, the so-called Chicago school (Davis, Havinghurst, Eells and others) has dealt with this problem rather extensively. For example, Davis (1) points out that the crucial problem involved in comparing the potential ability of two individuals to learn is one of determining the situations with which the two individuals have had equal experience. In order to arrive at an uncontaminated measure of capacity, it is essential to equalize such factors as cultural experience, training, and motivation.

Can we build tests in which these background factors are equalized? This depends on the extent to which we can identify variables that give rise to bias. Some variables are relatively easy to identify, and their effects can be minimized. For example, it is a simple task to build a test that will not show a bias in favor of boys or girls. The test maker can determine, statistically, which items show a sex difference, and eliminate them from his test. Or he can select his items in such a fashion that each sex is favored equally.

However, other bias-producing variables are much more difficult to identify and to deal with statistically. Most test experts will agree that, up to the present time, efforts to construct a test in which differences in experiential background and motivation have little or no effect on test scores (a so-called "culture-free" test) have been unsuccessful. Indeed, a growing number of test specialists, in the light of recent research concerning the characteristics of the disadvantaged child, maintain that the construction of a culture-free test is not possible.

What are some of the characteristics of the disadvantaged child that will tend to affect his test performance, and which must be taken into consideration by the test maker who seeks to build a culture-free test? Fishman (2) has summarized some of these characteristics. He points out that, in contrast to the middle-class child, the disadvantaged child will tend to be "less verbal, more fearful of strangers, less self-confident, less motivated toward scholastic and academic achievements, less competitive in the intellectual realm . . . , more apt to be bilingual, less exposed to intellectually stimulating materials in the home, less varied in recreational outlets, less knowledgeable about the world outside his immediate neighborhood, and more likely to attend inferior schools."

Note the difference between these characteristics and the boy-girl dichotomy that has been discussed. Here, we are dealing, in large measure, with attitudinal and motivational factors that substantially influence performance on intelligence tests, but which, unfortunately, cannot be "equalized" through statistical manipulation. In all probability, tests can be built that are more "equal" than those in common use at the present time, but the utility of such tests, particularly in the school situation, would be questionable. This brings us to our second problem.

THE PROBLEM OF PREDICTION

Why do we give intelligence tests? What is their function in the school situation? Essentially, the school is a mass educational enterprise that has as its goal the full development of each pupil. Intelligence tests provide a basis for grouping pupils in terms of their potential success in mastering school work; in that sense, they serve an important role in the individualization of instruction. They aid in the diagnosis of learning difficulties. The child who had difficulty in coping with school work may simply not be bright enough to cope with the demands placed upon him. On the other hand, tests also serve a valuable purpose by enabling the teacher to identify the child whose school work is below the level of his abilities

The intelligence test is a tool that helps the teacher establish reasonable goals for her pupil. It serves as a means of checking her estimates concerning his present level of performance, and of predicting his probable rate of progress—if the test is not affected by uncontrolled cultural factors. (And we are back to the question of bias again.)

Let us consider this point a bit more fully. If we accept the mass of research in the field—and accept it we must—cultural factors are important determiners of an individual's behavior. In that case, why should the influence of cultural factors be eliminated from intelligence tests, which are designed to sample and predict such behavior? There is no easy answer to this question; it depends on the extent to which the criteria that are used to validate the test are affected by cultural factors.

For example, suppose an intelligence test included a series of items which called for familiarity with Jack and Jill, Mary and her lamb, and Jack Sprat. If these items were administered to a cultural group in which these concepts were unknown, the validity of the test would certainly be lowered. However, suppose the test includes a series of items which call for facility in the use of English, and a given cultural group shows poor performance on these items. In this instance, the validity of the test would probably not be lowered, because the same factor that lowered the test score would also handicap the members of the group in their school progress, as well as in many other aspects of their daily life. The same thing is true of many other factors, such as motivation, self-confidence, interest in abstract ideas, fearfulness, which are likely to affect not only test performance, but a relatively extensive area of criterion behavior.

Disadvantaged groups tend to fare poorly on tests of intelligence, but it is foolhardy to assume that such intelligence as they possess has simply been overlaid by a concealing cloak of cultural factors, and that all we have to do is to peel off the cover and true intelligence would be revealed. To be sure, it is possible to construct tests that are less reflective of cultural factors than others. Unfortunately, such more "culturally fair" tests are not particularly useful in predicting success in school work. As far as the school is concerned, making a test culture-fair (reducing its bias) is of little value if, at the same time, the test's criterion validity is reduced. There is little point in using a test in the school situation that does not provide a good assessment or prediction of success in mastery of instructional goals, however socially worthy such a test might be.

The remedy must be sought not in the construction of new intelligence tests nor, as the New York City schools have done, in the elimination of all intelligence testing. Rather, the attack must be focused on the elimination of inequalities in opportunities for learning. This is the only way in which bias in the criterion, as well as in the test, can be reduced, and the only way in which better prediction can be attained.

THE PROBLEM OF OVER—GENERALIZATION

Education in America has been characterized by a band-wagon approach—our schools have consistently been guilty of over-emphasizing a worthwhile development. Remember the testing movement of the late twenties, when the standard test became, in the minds of many, the panacea for all educational ills? Remember the stress upon the role of social studies in the curriculum during the middle thirties, when the architects from Teachers College were going to use the schools to build a new social order? And remember the forties, when the schools were deluged by courses in meteorology, in radio, in aviation, and in navigation? The refresher course was in its heyday, and in a few weeks, social studies teachers were transformed into teachers of physics. And we must not forget the late fifties, when a new call to action was sounded by the Rickovers. The schools were called upon to meet the challenge of Sputnik, and development of programs for gifted children became the order of the day.

Now in the sixties, the calliope is sounding again, and the schools are being urged to meet another challenge— that of the culturally deprived, the culturally different, the culturally disadvantaged child. Once again, the voice of the barker is heard throughout the land, and he calls on the schools to take up the fight against a new enemy—the "slum" child.

Slum children, as described by the present day alarmist, all come from broken homes, characterized by lack of adult supervision, drug addiction, alcoholism, prostitution, disease, high mobility, and all other concomitants of poverty. These other-side-of-the-track children, coming from homes where there is little verbal, sensory, or experiential stimulation, are forced into middle-class oriented schools, where they are taught by middle-class teachers who do not understand them.

And because they do poorly, they are relegated to classes for slow learners where they receive inferior schooling. Even the standardized tests that they take, as Haggard (3) puts it, are "saturated with middle-class vocabulary and language forms, and . . . the experiences and knowledges tested are those with which most middle-class children are relatively familiar." This, of course, is understandable—the tests are constructed by "middle-class individuals, buttressed by middle-class experiences, ways of thinking, and language forms," who often standardize their tests in terms of . . . middle class values."

Of course, it is impossible to deny the wealth of statistical evidence that is available concerning the incidence of social pathology among culturally disadvantaged groups in the United States today. But one must guard against the fallacy of over-generalization, of classifying all slum children as if they were a homogeneous group. Within the broad group characterized as culturally disadvantaged, there are many families whose inner resources enable them to combat the effects of slum living. The children of these families reflect the inner strength of their homes in their performance in school and in their adjustment to society as a whole.

Perhaps the results of a recent study (4) of intelligence test and achievement test scores of disadvantaged children might serve to indicate the dangers involved in over-generalization concerning such children. The data analyzed in this study were drawn from the record cards of a group of 934 pupils who were attending 16 schools located in disadvantaged areas in New York City.

Each of the pupils involved met the following criteria: (1) they had entered the New York City schools for the first time either in kindergarten or first grade; (2) they showed uninterrupted attendance in the regular grades of the New York City public schools—none of the children had left the school system and returned to it at any time during the period and none had been enrolled in special classes (health conservation classes, hospital classes, etc.) at any time; and (3) their record cards indicated that they had taken the Otis Alpha Intelligence Test at the third-grade level and the Otis Beta Intelligence Test at the sixth-grade level. In addition, scores on the appropriate level of the Metropolitan Reading Test given in the third and sixth grades were available for 885 of the pupils covered in the study.

Data were also gathered concerning the total number of times each of the pupils had been admitted to a different public school in the city. Of the total group of 934 pupils, 395 (42.3 per cent) had attended only one school. The record cards of the remaining pupils indicated that they had attended two or more schools during the first six years. Indeed, one pupil had been enrolled in 15 different elementary schools between the first and sixth grades. For the purposes of this study, any pupil who showed more than a single admission to a New York City public school was considered a "mobil" pupil.

Virtually no change in IQ from third to sixth grade was noted for the total group of 934 pupils. However, when the total group was divided into two subgroups, a stable subgroup that had been enrolled in a single elementary school for its entire schooling and a mobile subgroup that had attended more than one elementary school during the six-year period, sharp differences were observed. In the case of the stable subgroup, a mean rise of 1.6 IQ points was obtained; in the case of the mobile subgroup, a mean drop of 1.3 IQ points was noted. In both instances, the mean difference between third and sixth grade IQ was statictically significant.

The changes noted in reading grade scores showed much the same pattern as those noted for IQ's. The total group of disadvantaged pupils performed 3.4 months below grade level on Test I—Word Knowledge when they were tested in the third grade. On the sixth-grade level, their performance was 2.8 months below grade level. The total group was 5.3 months below grade level on Test II—Reading when they were in the third grade; in the sixth grade, they were 3.6 months below grade level. Not only was there no drop in performance over the three year period, but the pupils showed a slight gain in functioning relative to grade level. In the case of Test II, the gain of 1.7 months was statistically significant.

Here, too, sharp differences arose when the non-mobile subgroup (pupils who had attended a single elementary school during the six-year period) was contrasted with the mobile subgroup (pupils who attended more than one school). The non-mobile subgroup showed a gain of three months relative to grade on Test I and of approximately four months relative to grade on Test II, between the third and sixth grades. Both gains were statistically significant. The mobile subgroup showed a loss of 1.4 months relative to grade on Test I and no change on Test II. The drop on Test I was statistically significant.

Clearly, there is a marked difference when we compare stable and mobile subgroups among the larger disadvantaged group. Note particularly the considerable error that is involved when only the data for the total group are considered, and generalizations are advanced solely on the basis of such total group data.

THE PROBLEM OF TEST INTERPRETATION

Tests are perhaps the most important tools that educators have at their disposal for assessing and predicting pupil performance. It is unfortunate that, too often, they are used so routinely and so mechanically that critics of tests have little difficulty in pointing to instances in which test results have been misinterpreted.

Consider a hypothetical case. Suppose a doctor weighs a disadvantaged youngster who has been on a substandard diet for several years and finds that he tips the scales at 85 pounds, about 15 pounds below normal for his age. To the health practitioner, this weight would be looked upon as one of a number of descriptive facts about the child, and would be used as a bench mark for determining improvement in the child's nutritional status following the institution of a program designed to overcome the deficiencies in his diet.

Now suppose a school gives a standardized intelligence test to this same child, and finds that he has an IQ of 85, about 15 points below "normal." Too often, this IQ is looked upon as equivalent to the IQ of 85 obtained by a native-born middle-class youngster, and the disadvantaged youngster is routinely assigned to a low level group. Rather, this IQ should serve, as the substandard weight, as a bench mark for judging the progress made after the organization of a remedial program designed to overcome existing deficiencies.

Test scores, like any other items of information, may be erroneous—even when they are correct, they may be subject to misinterpretation—but the remedy is not to eliminate the test, but to develop means of using test information with greater understanding. Eliminating the test is comparable to throwing away the soap with the wash water.

CONCLUSION

What, then, can be done to solve some of these problems? In large measure, what is needed, particularly insofar as schools are concerned, is a massive educational program concerning the uses and limitations of intelligence tests. Teachers and school administrators must be taught that test scores are not fixed, absolute quantities reflecting some native endowment. They must learn to look upon test scores as a tool; they must learn to evaluate the behavior of the child, as well as his scores. What does it mean if a disadvantaged child ranks low on the vocabulary section of a scholastic aptitude test, yet shows a considerable degree of facility in verbal interchanges with his peers?

It is important, too, that comparisons with others be minimized. To be sure, at times one would want to compare the test scores of disadvantaged and advantaged children, if only to determine the extent of the handicap which called for remedial measures. At other times, one would want to determine the relative standing of a disadvantaged child within the cultural group of which he is a member. Most often, however, the test score of a disadvantaged child must be looked upon as a base for judging the adequacy of the school's program.

Failure to realize that the disadvantaged child may not have had the background of experiences that will enable him to cope with a given test; failure to realize that he is not as motivated to do well on tests as advantaged children; failure to realize that a host of predisposing home and family factors serve as distracting influences when tests are administered—these failures are symptomatic of lack of professional awareness, and can be overcome by a program designed to foster professional competence. Using inappropriate tests or misinterpreting test results, whether one is dealing with a group of disadvantaged children, or any other children, represents professional immaturity. The schools must accept the responsibility of making sure that tests are used wisely and well, and train teachers and administrators to that end. Only then will the schools be able to say that they have met their responsibility of helping the disadvantaged child become a responsible, contributing member of society.

References

Davis, Allison, *Social Class Influences upon Learning* (Boston: Harvard University Press, 1948).

Fishman, Joshua A., (Editor), "Guidelines for Testing Minority Group Children," *Journal of Social Issues*, Vol. 20 (1964), pp. 127-145.

Haggard, Ernest A., "Influence of Culture Background on Test Performance," *Proceedings, 1949 Invitational Conference on Testing Problems* (Princeton, N. J.: Educational Testing Service, 1950).

Justman, Joseph, "Stability of Academic Aptitude and Achievement Test Scores of Mobile Disadvangaged Children." (Unpublished paper).

17. On Telling Parents About Test Results

James H. Ricks, Jr.

Like any other organization dealing with people, a school has many confidences to keep. School administrators, teachers, and especially guidance workers inevitably come to know items of private information. A gossip who carelessly passes such information around abuses his position and his relationship with his students. It is both right and important that some kinds of information be kept in confidence.

What about test results? Do they belong in the category of secrets, to be seen only by professional eyes and mentioned only in whispers? Or is their proper function best served when they become common knowledge in the school and its community? (In some towns, names and scores have been listed in the local newspaper, much like the results of an athletic contest.)

We think neither extreme is a good rule. Sometimes there is reason to make group data—figures such as the average and the range from high to low—generally public. Seldom should individual results be published except for the happy announcement of a prize won, a scholarship awarded, and the like. But short of general publication, school guidance workers face a particularly important question: Should parents be told their children's test results?

Hard questions, often, are hard because they deal with genuinely complicated problems. Simple "solutions" to such questions are likely to be a trap rather

From *Test Service Bulletin,* Number 54, 1959, by James H. Ricks, Jr. Reprinted with consent of the Psychological Corporation, New York.

than an aid if their effect is to divert our attention from the difficulties we truly face. Simple rules or principles, on the other hand, can be of real help as one tackles complex problems and situations. This article will present some rules that we have found useful in facing questions such as—

"What should I say when a mother wants to know her son's IQ?" "Should we send aptitude test profiles home with the children?" "We feel that parents in our school ought to know the results of the achievement tests we give, but then it's hard to explain the discrepancies between these and the teachers' grades."

No single procedure, obviously, can be appropriate for every kind of test. Nor for every kind of parent. To Mr. Jones, a well-adjusted and well-educated father, a report of his daughter's test scores may enhance his understanding of her capacities and of what the school has been giving her. To Mr. Green, a somewhat insecure and less knowledgeable man, the identical information may spark an explosion damaging to both child and school. And the counselor or teacher often has no sure way of knowing which kind of person he will be reporting to.

Two principles and one verbal technique seem to us to provide a sound basis for communicating the information obtained from testing. The two "commandments" are absolutely interdependent—without the second the first is empty, and without the first the second is pointless.

The first: PARENTS HAVE THE RIGHT TO KNOW WHATEVER THE SCHOOL KNOWS ABOUT THE ABILITIES, THE PERFORMANCE, AND THE PROBLEMS OF THEIR CHILDREN.

The second: THE SCHOOL HAS THE OBLIGATION TO SEE THAT IT COMMUNICATES UNDERSTANDABLE AND USABLE KNOWLEDGE. Whether by written report or be individual conference, the school must make sure it is giving *real* information—not just the illusion of information that bare numbers or canned interpretations often afford. And the information must be in terms that parents can absorb and use.

Few educators will dispute the first principle. It is in parents that the final responsibility for the upbringing and education of the children must lie. This responsibility requires access to all available information bearing on educational and vocational decisions to be made for and by the child. The school is the agent to which parents have delegated part of the educational process— but the responsibility has been delegated, not abdicated. Thoughtful parents do not take these responsibilities and rights lightly.

The parents' right to know, then, we regard as indisputable. But, to know what?

Suppose that, as a result of judicious testings, the school knows that Sally has mastered social studies and general science better than many in her ninth grade class, but that few do as poorly as she in math. In English usage she stands about in the middle, but her reading level is barely up to the lower border of the students who successfully complete college preparatory work in her high school. The best prediction that can be made of her probable scores on the College Boards three years hence is that they will fall in the range which makes her eligible for the two-year community college, but not for the university. She grasps mechanical concepts better than most boys, far better than most girls. Looking over the test results and her records, her experienced teacher recognizes that good habits and neatness of work have earned Sally grades somewhat better than would be expected from her test scores.

All of these are things Sally's parents should know. Will they know them if they are given the numbers— Sally's IQ score, percentiles for two reading scores, percentiles on another set of norms for several aptitude tests, and grade-placement figures on an achievement battery?[1]

Telling someone something he does not understand does not increase his knowledge (at least not his correct and usable knowledge—we are reminded of the guide's observation about the tenderfoot, "It ain't so much

---

[1] The implied "No" answer to this question does not, of course, refer to those few parents trained in psychometrics—perhaps even to a point beyond the training of the school staff. Parents include all kinds of people.

what he don't know, it's what he knows that ain't so that gits him in trouble"). Transmitting genuine knowledge requires attention to content, language, and audience. We have already referred to some of the characteristics of parents as an audience. Let's look at the other two elements.

Content means that to begin with, *we* must ourselves know what we are trying to get across.

We need to know just what evidence there is to show that the test results deserve any consideration at all. We need equally to know the margins and probabilities of error in predictions based on tests. If we don't know *both* what the scores mean *and* how much confidence may properly be placed in them, we are in trouble at the start—neither our own use of the information nor our transmission of it to others will be very good.

Content—what we are going to say—and *language*— how we are going to put it—are inseparable when we undertake to tell somebody something. In giving information about test results, we need to think about the general content and language we shall use and also about the specific terms we shall use.

To illustrate the general content-and-language planning: a guidance director may decide that he wants first to get across a sense of both the values and the weaknesses of test scores. One excellent device for his purpose would be an expectancy table or chart. Such a chart can make it clear to persons without training in statistics that test results are useful predictors *and* that the predictions will not always be precise. Local studies in one's own school or community are of greatest interest. But the guidance director who lacks local data may still find illustrative tables from other places helpful in preparing parents and students to use test results in a sensible way.

Specific terms used in expressing test results vary considerably in the problems they pose. Consider, for example, the different kinds of numbers in which test results may be reported.

IQ's are regarded as numbers that should rarely if ever be reported as such to students or to their parents. The reason is that an IQ is likely to be seen as a fixed characteristic of the person tested, as somehow something more than the test score it really represents. The effect, too often, is that of a final conclusion about the individual rather than that of a piece of information useful in further thinking and planning. Few things interfere more effectively with real understanding than indiscriminate reporting of IQ scores to parents.

GRADE PLACEMENT scores or STANDARD SCORES of various kinds are less likely to cause trouble than IQ scores are. Still, they may substitute an illusion of communication for real communication. Standard scores have no more meaning to most parents than raw scores unless there is opportunity for extensive explanations. Grade placements *seem* so simple and straightforward that serious misunderstandings may result from their use. As noted in a very helpful pamphlet,[2] a sixth-grade pupil with grade-placement scores of 10.0 for reading and 8.5 for arithmetic does not necessarily rank higher in reading than he does in arithmetic when compared to the other sixth-graders. (Both scores may be at the 95th percentile for his class—arithmetic progress much more than reading progress tends to be dependent on what has been taught, and thus to spread over a narrower range at any one grade.)

PERCENTILES probably are the safest and most informative numbers to use PROVIDED their two essential characteristics are made clear: (1) that they refer not to per cent of questions answered correctly but to per cent of people whose performance the student has equalled or surpassed, and (2) who, specifically, are the people with whom the student is being compared. The second point—a definite description of the comparison or "norm" group—is especially important in making the meaning of test results clear.

Much more can be said about the kinds of numbers used to convey test score information. Good discussions can be found in a number of textbooks.[3] But a more

---

[2]Katz, M. R. *Selecting an Achievement Test.* E. & A. Series No. 3, 1958 (Page 26). Available free from Educational Testing Service, Princeton, New Jersey.

[3]See, for example, Chapters 17 and 18 in *Measurement and Evaluation in Psychology and Education,* by Thorndike and Hagan (New York: Wiley, 1955), or pages 556–563 and 584–588 in *Appraising Vocational Fitness,* by Super (New York: Harper, 1949).

fundamental question remains—*are any numbers neces-sary?*

We intend nothing so foolish as suggesting a ban on the use of numbers in reporting test results. But we have been struck repeatedly by the fact that some of the very best counselors and many of the best written reports present numerical data only incidentally or not at all.

Along with the two "commandments" at the beginning of this article, we mentioned a verbal technique. Generally, we dislike formulas for writing or speaking. This one, however, seems to have advantages that outweigh the risks attending its suggestion. It's just a few words:

"YOU SCORE LIKE PEOPLE WHO . . ." Or, to a parent, "Your son (or daughter) scores like students who . . ."

The sentence, of course, requires completion. The completion depends on the test or other instrument, the reason for testing, and the person to whom the report is being given. Some sample completions:

"... people who are pretty good at office work, fast and accurate enough to hold a job and do it well."

"... people who don't find selling insurance a very satisfactory choice. Three out of four who score as you do and become insurance salesmen leave the job for something else in less than a year."

"... students who find getting into liberal arts college and getting a B.A. degree something they can attain only with extra hard work. On the other hand, they find a year or two of technical school interesting and they probably do well in the jobs to which that leads."

"... students who are disappointed later if they don't begin a language in the ninth grade and plan to take some more math and science. It's easier to head toward business later if you still want to than to go from the commercial course into a good college."

"... students who don't often—only about one out of four—manage to earn a C average their freshman year at State."

"... students who have more than average difficulty passing in arithmetic—you [*or, to a parent,* he] may need some extra help on this in the next few years."

Many more samples will come readily to mind. The most important thing to note is that a satisfactory report combines two kinds of information:

1. the test results of the individual person, and
2. Something known about the test or battery and its relationship to the subsequent performance of others who have taken it.

Also, a satisfactory completion puts the school or the counselor out on a limb, at least a little. Some variant of "That's not so!" or, more politely, "How do you know?" will be the reaction in some cases, probably less frequently voiced than it is felt.

Well, let's face it. The decision to use a test at all is a step out on a limb. Some limbs are broad and solid and the climber need feel little or no anxiety. Some are so frail that they offer only hazard, with the bait of an improbable reward. We climb out on some limbs of medium safety because there is evidence of a real chance that they will help us, and those whom we test, toward a worthwhile goal.

The words of the formula need not actually be used in each case. Sometimes percentiles, grade placement scores, or a profile may be what the parents should receive. But it is well to try first mentally stating the meaning of the results in the language suggested above. If this proves difficult or discomforting, a warning signal is on—reporting the numbers is likely not to be constructive in the case at hand!

The audience of parents to which our test-based information is to be transmitted includes an enormous range and variety of minds and emotions. Some are ready and able to absorb what we have to say. Reaching others may be as hopeless as reaching TV watchers with an AM radio broadcast. Still others may hear what we say, but clothe the message with their own special needs, ideas, and predilections.

The habit of using the formula, and of thinking a bit about what answer to give if the response is a challenging or doubting one, puts the interpreter of test scores in the strongest position he can occupy. In the case of achievement tests, it requires him to understand why and how the particular test or battery was chosen as appropriate for his school and his purpose. In the case of aptitude (including scholastic aptitude or intelligence) tests, it requires him to examine the evidence offered in the test manual and research studies to back up the test's claim to usefulness. And it reminds him always that it is in the end *his* thinking, *his* weighing of the evidence, *his* soundness and helpfulness as an educator or counselor that is exposed for judgment—not the sometimes wistful ideas of the test author or publisher.

The school—or the counselor—*is* exposed for judgment when telling parents about the abilities and performances of their children. The parents have the right to know. And knowledge in terms they can understand and absorb is what the school must give.

18. What Mental Tests Really Tell About Your Youngster

Hillel Black

Attempting to predict future performance on the basis of test scores is much like trying to guess the ultimate size and shape of an oak tree by measuring a sapling in pitch darkness with a rubber band for a ruler, without taking into account the condition of the soil, the amount of rainfall or the woodsman's axe. The amazing thing is that sometimes we get the right answer.

David Goslin of Russell Sage Foundation
in *The Search for Ability*

Here are three questions from as many different tests. All may be said to define something called intelligence. See if you can surmise what it is they attempt to measure.

1. The following is from an I.Q. test given to three-month-old babies.

> An infant is held in an upright position before a table. A teaspoon is then placed within his easy view and may be tapped or moved about to attract his attention. Does the child's eyes remain on the spoon or return to it after the examiner has removed his hand?

(Credit is given if the child continues to look at the spoon.)

2. This question comes from the Iowa Tests of Educational Development, which are widely used in the nation's high schools.

From *They Shall Not Pass* by Hillel Black. Reprinted by permission of William Morrow & Co., Inc. Copyright © 1963 by Hillel Black.

What is a trial jury?

(1) A court decision.
(2) A crime for which a man is tried.
(3) A promise to tell the truth and the truth only.
(4) A body of people who hear evidence and are
    expected to bring in a verdict.

(The correct choice is No. 4.)

3. The final example is taken from the Scholastic
Aptitude Test.

Select the lettered pair of words which best ex-
presses a relationship similar to that expressed in the
original pair.

SNUB: CONTEMPT::

(A) injury:retaliation
(B) applause:approbation
(C) praise:understanding
(D) scorn:superiority
(E) grimace:amusement

(The correct choice is B.)

The questions you have just read illustrate three
mental processes. The first shows awareness and percep-
tion, the second calls for remembered fact, the third
involves reasoning whereby the student must discern a
relationship in seemingly unrelated concepts. In effect,
we have found that intelligence consists of not one thing
but many components. The truth is that no one knows
how many. When the French physician Alfred Binet
introduced the first formal intelligence scale for children
in 1905 he believed there were eleven. An Englishman,
C. E. Spearman, thought there was only one general
intelligence factor. And an American, E. L. Thorndike,
concluded that there were as many different kinds of
intelligence processes as one cared to name.

One of the great paradoxes of testing is that while no
one knows precisely what intelligence is, certain kinds
of intelligence can be measured on tests, however
imprecisely. One of the reasons educational tests work
at all is that they take a narrow view of intelligence; that
is, they measure only a limited number of mental
abilities.

As we have already seen, intelligence and aptitude tests tell us little if anything about the mental traits necessary to compose music, create a sonnet or produce an original philosophical thought. What they do measure are some basic aptitudes associated with learning. Thus it is possible to measure in a limited fashion your child's ability to learn mathematics by giving him mathematical problems to solve. It is also possible to measure his ability to learn history (or literature, philosophy, science) by asking him to read selected passages in the subjects and then questioning how well he comprehends what he has read. The reason this type of test happens to be somewhat effective is that the primary way people learn any of these subjects is by reading books, articles and documents.

It is not surprising, then, that most of the 100 million standardized tests given annually in the nation's elementary and high schools as well as several million college entrance and scholarship exams generally measure three basic intelligence traits or aptitudes: *memory, verbal* and *numerical ability* (also called mathematical). These exams are of two kinds: scholastic aptitude or intelligence tests and achievement tests. The scholastic or intelligence tests stress verbal and mathematical skills learned over *a long period of time.* Achievement tests are usually devoted to specific subjects, such as chemistry or French, and emphasize knowledge learned over a *short period* of time.

This brings us to an essential point. All educational tests ATTEMPT to do the same thing, *measure your youngster's academic ability and thereby predict the kinds of grades he will get in school.* In other words, they *TRY to forecast future academic performance.* Two key words are "attempt" and "try," for as we shall soon see, all educational tests make only very approximate measures of your son's or daughter's mental capacity. Moreover, no educational test—and this includes I.Q. tests—can predict success in a career. While there are standardized tests that aid in forecasting whether your child has the ability to learn law, medicine or engineering, they cannot predict whether he will make an intelligent or successful lawyer, physician or engineer.

We have attempted to show *what* educational tests *attempt* to measure, but we have yet to show *how* they determine mental capacity. For example, a score of 600 on the SAT is obviously higher than a score of 400. But what does this mean? What does it tell you and the college your youngster chooses about his ability to learn? And how accurate are these tests in measuring your child's academic intelligence or scholastic aptitude?

To answer these crucial questions, we can begin by turning to an unlikely source, the Book of Judges, which describes one of the first standardized tests ever given. This Old Testament exam predates testing as we know it by some twenty centuries. Here is the exam as described in the Bible:

> And the Gileadites took the passages of Jordan before the Ephraimites: and it was so, that when those Ephraimites which were escaped said, Let me go over; that the men of Gilead said unto him, Art thou an Ephraimite? If he said, Nay;
> Then said they unto him, Say now Shibboleth; and he said Sibboleth: for he could not frame to pronounce it right. Then they took him, and slew him at the passages of Jordan: and there fell at that time of the Ephraimites forty and two thousand. (Judges 12:5,6).

For those who feel overwhelmed by the pressures of modern testing, there is always the consolation that the current penalties for failure are decidedly less severe. However, this grim little quiz of the Gileadites serves another purpose. Though obviously not a test of mental ability, it illustrates several things about how modern mass testing works.

Unwittingly, the men of Gilead employed the two basic principles of all standardized tests used today. The first principle is that every test consists of a fraction of the possible samples of human thought or behavior which the test taker is asked to perform. The Gileadites could have required each enemy soldier to describe at great length Gileadite customs, history and religion. Instead they posed one sample question. They were then able to distinguish friend from foe because the Ephraimites could not pronounce the *sh* sound in "Shibboleth."

The second Gileadite principle may be called the principle of comparison. By comparing how two different groups responded to the same question—Ephraimite *vs.* Gileadite pronunciation—the victors identified the enemy.

This is a distillation of the morass of words written about psychometrics, or mental measurement. Summarized in one sentence: *Standardized testing compares the different ways people perfrom an identical series of tasks.*

Now let us see what testing can do for your child. Suppose you want to measure your child's scholastic aptitude. Even though you can't peer inside his brain and see his ability, you know it is there. Your son consistently obtains A's and B's while others make C's or F's. What we have just said is that one way to measure scholastic ability or aptitude is through teachers' judgments of what teachers like to think are real-life performances in school over a long period of time.

Another way to measure your youngster's scholastic aptitude is to give him a test. Like the Ephraimites who had to pronounce the word "Shibboleth," this will be only a *sample* performance. Unlike a year's classroom quizzes, essays and recitations, the test will be extremely limited in the number and kinds of tasks your boy will be asked to perform. Most tests measuring any kind of aptitude, such as understanding the meaning of words or the ability to do math, contain fewer than 50 questions.

You can now see why school grades are better than test scores in predicting your child's future academic performance. Not only do grades represent many more and different tasks than questions asked on tests, but these school tasks are performed over a long period of time and hence are a measure of the willingness to work or study. As we have already seen even among geniuses, a key trait is the willingness to persevere.

But an even more crucial point is that every standardized test, because it represents only a *highly limited sample* of ability, must by its nature be an inherently inaccurate measure of your youngster's capabilities. This has a profound meaning for your child. It means that no standardized test he will ever take can tell you or his teachers precisely how much chemistry or biology he knows or just how much verbal or mathematical aptitude he possesses.

A simple example will suffice. Suppose you want to know how many words your thirteen-year-old daughter can spell. The best way to find out is to give her a test containing all the words in the English language. But such a task is highly impractical. Instead she is given a test that contains 50 carefully selected words graded according to difficulty. As chance would have it, your child knows only ten of these words. But suppose she had been given a similar list with 50 other words and could spell nearly all of them. It would be just a matter of luck that she was given the first list instead of the second. It is this kind of luck, good or bad depending on how your youngster does, that inherently makes all standardized tests imprecise measurements of a child's ability. Summed up, these inaccuracies are due to the limited sample taken of each aptitude.

Carry this thought one step further. What does this mean in terms of the score your child receives? Let us suppose your daughter obtains a 120 I.Q. This is not her "true" score, that hypothetical mark she would have received if she had been asked all the aptitude questions that man could think up. Instead, it is only an approximate estimate of her intelligence quotient. This means that at the time your youngster took the test her "true" score probably fell within a range of 110 I.Q. to 130 I.Q. Indeed, the range could be even greater.

Now let us apply the first principle of testing we have culled from the Book of Judges to the most crucial college admission exam your child is likely to take, the verbal section of the Scholastic Aptitude Test. What happens when the SAT tests only a *limited sample* of your youngster's aptitudes?

This test, as you will recall, is rated on a scale from 200 to 800. Assume your son obtained a score of 480 on the SAT-Verbal, which happens to be about average for those taking the test and thus is the score most youngsters achieve. Is 480 his "true" score? What does this indicate in terms of his ability to do college work?

It is possible because of this incomplete or limited sample of your youngster's verbal abilities that his "true" score lies somewhere near 360, which only the *bottom* 15 per cent of college-bound students obtain. It is also possible that his "true" score—what he is truly capable of doing—is near 600, which only the *top* 15 per cent or the very superior students achieve. Simply put, it is possible that your boy's obtained score is no measure of his verbal aptitude. According to the test, he may be an academic dunderhead or extremely capable in the use and understanding of words. The chances of such a large range of error occurring are extremely slim—roughly one out of 10,000. The important thing is that it can happen.

What is much more likely to happen is that your son's "true" score will fall between 420 and 540.* To say it another way, if his "true" score is 420, it is possible that his verbal aptitude or intelligence is just a little better than the *bottom* 25 per cent of college-bound seniors who took the test. But if his "true" score is 540, his verbal aptitude may be better than roughly 75 per cent of all those high school seniors who took the SAT. If your boy obtains an average score on the SAT-Verbal he may be quite limited in verbal academic ability, including the ability to read with understanding. It is also just as possible that he is quite exceptional. The only thing you and his schoolteachers can be fairly sure of is that he is neither a total dunce nor a quiz kid.

Besides the inherent errors in all tests owing to a limited sample of abilities, there are other inaccuracies which can prove equally harmful to your child if his scores are not interpreted with extreme caution. Now let us see precisely what can happen when different people's aptitudes are compared, which is the second basic principle of all modern testing.

"About 40 years ago," John Dobbin of ETS declared, "there appeared in our folklore the notion that an I.Q. is something one *has,* like large feet or a bass voice—and

---

*Assuming your son took the SAT 100 times, there are 95 chances that his "true" score would fall within a 120–point range. The test makers call this range estimate the standard error of measurement, which is due to the inherent error in tests because they are only limited samples of ability.

there is nothing to be done about it. Furthermore, according to the folklore, some very psychological tests can be used to tell you just exactly how much of this I.Q. you have, only you must never know how much if you have a lot, because it will warp your perspective, nor how little, if you have very little, because you will become discouraged. And this odd notion has remained current to this day, even—nay, particularly—among educated people. I wish we could somehow throw away the whole I.Q. concept—blot it out of our records, our textbooks, and our recollection—for it stands in the way of our properly understanding young people and how they mature."

As John Dobbin notes, there is really nothing holy about the I.Q. or intelligence quotient. It is simply a test score or symbol for how well somebody did on a particular intelligence test. The only way a test maker can describe your child's intelligence is by comparing his test score with others. It is similar to measuring a child's height. Is he tall for his age, average or below average? This same principle of comparison is used in testing.

To illustrate: Your youngster is ten years old. He takes an intelligence test and does as well as the *average* twelve-year-old. In other words, on this particular intelligence test he has shown that he possesses a *mental age* of twelve. Now you want to find out what his I.Q. is. You simply divide his *mental age* by his *chronological* or actual age (12 divided by 10 equals 1.2) and then multiply by 100. This means your child has obtained a 120 I.Q. Because the average I.Q. is generally 100, it would appear that your youngster is above average in academic intelligence.

But how precise is this score which happens to be called an Intelligence Quotient? Would he have received a different I.Q. if he had taken another test? The answers may surprise you.

To obtain a range of test scores that have any meaning, test makers must try them out or standardize them on a population of above-average, average and below-average ability. Certainly the ideal would be to standardize or try out a test on, say, all teen-agers in the United States. But such a task is obviously impossible.

So instead the test makers supposedly pick what they believe is a representative sample. The only trouble is that their so-called sample is never truly representative and often doesn't even exist.

To illustrate, suppose your youngster took the individually administered Stanford-Binet intelligence test. What would his probable "equivalent" I.Q. be if he had taken the following group intelligence tests?

If he obtained a Binet I.Q. of 168 and took the	His probable I.Q. would be
Kuhlman-Anderson	170
Henmon-Nelson	160
California Test of Mental Maturity	148
Otis	142

Incredibly, we find that if your youngster had taken the Otis instead of the Kuhlmann-Anderson he might have been "penalized" 28 I.Q. points. These possible "penalties" decrease to 16 points at the 140 I.Q. level of the Binet and to 13 I.Q. points at the 115 I.Q. level.

In effect, your youngster's Intelligence Quotient might increase appreciably if he were given a different publisher's test. In other words, the I.Q. he obtains may depend largely on the test he takes. Moreover, these differences in I.Q. scores can be crucial for many college-bound youngsters, admissions officers and elementary and high school guidance advisers and teachers. The question is: Do school officials who guide and place your child on the basis of I.Q.'s know these differences exist?

How, you may wonder, could these "errors" in measurement occur? And they do affect nearly all standardized tests—I.Q., aptitude or achievement. John Dobbin supplies the answer.

"Some of the variation," he says, "is due to the nature of the tests themselves (perhaps the sampling of intellectual skill is too narrow or too small in one or another of them); some of it is due to the nature of the human beings who are measured (no one ever reacts in exactly the same way to a test on successive occasions); and a great deal of it is due to differences in the populations on which tests have been built and normed [standardized] ."

Publishers of most tests, he adds, talk about a "national norm" and encourage the users of their tests to believe that they can compare the scores of their own students against a scale that represents a national average of scores. "This is a vicious delusion," he declares, "for there is no such thing as a national norm for any test. There never has been such a thing—there is not now, and probably never will be.

"Most publishers, for very compelling economic reasons, seek to have their standardizations partially paid for by the sale of the test materials at a reduced price. They offer to sell the tests to the schools for the cost of printing (25-50 per cent of the usual list price) if the schools will return test papers or scores for use in the computation of norms. So now we have norms based on 'children in schools that use tests and are willing to buy this particular test.' And the end is not yet.

"In order to obtain a sample that is large enough to impress the public, or larger than a competitor's sample, most publishers seek to sell these reduced-price tests for norming to larger school systems. . . . So here we have the population the publisher samples to get his 'national norm'—[i.e.] 12-year-olds in school, in schools that use tests, in schools that will buy *this* test, mostly in cities of 100,000 population or more. What the publisher obtains from that population, even if he samples it very carefully, is not a 'national norm.' "

In effect, if your youngster takes a standardized English, science or general intelligence test, he does not obtain an English score, science score or an absolute I.Q. Because of the varying contents of the tests and the different populations on which every test is standardized, he earns a score that is truly meaningful only in relation to the specific test he took. In fact, says John Dobbin, sometimes the best you can say is that he earns a score on "a particular edition of a particular test."

The consequence of what you have read so far is the incontestable fact that educational testing, despite its statistical refinements, remains a crude measurement of academic capacity. You can never say this is your youngster's "true" score—his absolute and final I.Q. or his absolute and final College Board score. Because his score must be interpreted within a fairly broad range, he may be much more or less academically capable than his test score indicates. Furthermore, the only point where standardized tests become truly successful in separating ability are at the extremes. Thus a standardized test is most likely to work well when it attempts to separate a moron, a person of average intelligence and an academic genius. And even in separating the lower orders of intelligence from the middle and the middle from the top, mental tests frequently fail to make even partially accurate distinctions. Finally, it should be stressed that how well your youngster does on a particular standardized exam depends upon the mental maturity he has achieved up to the moment he took the test.

Another myth found in our folklore is that children's intelligence does not change or grow. On the contrary, it grows at different rates, with some aptitudes developing faster than others, like height and weight. Moreover, some mental abilities seem to stop growing for a while and then suddenly spurt ahead.

Again let us take the I.Q. as an illustration. Nancy Bayley, who conducted a pioneering eighteen-year-long study, discovered all this when she showed the variations in intelligence that occur during childhood. Dr. Bayley found that the mean I.Q. of the group she surveyed was a little over 103 at one month. But by the time these children had reached eighteen years of age their mean I.Q. had increased to 122. Even more important, a child's intelligence has its ups and downs, which are most marked during infancy and the first year of adolescence. One youngster's intelligence quotient ranged from 115 at three, 155 at ten, 119 at thirteen, to 135 at eighteen. Declared Dr. Bayley: "Although many children maintain fairly constant levels of intelligence after six years of age, in some there are wide shifts in mental level. These shifts may occur at any age, and over a wide range of intellectual ability."

What does all this mean for your youngster? Standardized tests are simply another tool of aiding you and your child's teachers in predicting his ability to learn in school. Taken alone, they are worthless and dangerous.

However, when test scores are added to school grades they often improve the forecast of your child's capability of doing college work or learning mathematics or science or any other academic subject.

The only way tests should be used as an aid in making these forecasts is to employ a prediction index that combines both a child's test scores and his previous grades. The individual prediction index that appears below is typical of the kind used by Ivy League colleges and others as their main tool in deciding whether a youngster will be admitted.

This particular prediction index is based on Scholastic Aptitude Test scores and high school grades. Students are ranked in three groups. The *top* group consists of students with high grade averages and high test scores. The *middle* rank is made up of students with average grades and scores; the *bottom*, low grades and scores. The question this prediction index attempts to answer is: What freshman grades are students likely to obtain at the end of their first year in college?

Expectancy Table for Predicting Academic
Success of College Freshmen

Prediction Index	Per cent failing in college	Per cent between failing and a B in college	Per cent getting B or better in college
Top-ranking high school students	0	5	95
Middle-ranking high school students	10	53	37
Bottom-ranking high school students	65	35	0

What this table says is that a top-ranking student who has displayed his scholastic brilliance in high school and scored high on the SAT has 95 chances out of 100 of making a B record or better and 5 chances in 100 of doing middling well in his freshman year. Conversely, a bottom-ranking student has no apparent chance of getting a B or better and 35 chances out of 100 of just getting by. (Actually, it is possible for a top-ranking student to fail and a bottom-ranking student to obtain honors. There are always exceptions because of all the inherent errors already described in tests as well as the fallibility of grades as a measurement of ability.)

It is with the middle-ranking students that the prediction problem becomes acute. A glance at the table makes this immediately clear. As with the top and bottom, it is impossible to forecast whether your child—if he is middle rank—will fail, pass or obtain honors.

Nevertheless, the individual prediction index is a marked improvement over grades *or* test scores used alone in forecasting a child's ability to learn. Without doubt, it is the basic tool that gives tests any practical meaning. It can be employed by school principals, psychologists, teachers and counselors as an aid in placing youngsters in fast, average or slow classes. It can be used by admission officers to cut down the risks of possible dropouts who are unable to make the grade. And finally it can be used by guidance advisers as one estimate of a child's chances of succeeding in a particular college or high school track.

Yet it is one of the supreme ironies of how tests are used that only a handful of the more competitive colleges will tell high schools how their individual prediction indices work. Of the more than 600 members of the College Board, only four—Tulane, Women's College at North Carolina, the University of Oregon and Penn State—send their prediction tables to high schools that seek them. Thus it is virtually impossible for even an informed high school guidance counselor to do more than offer a crude interpretation of what a student's College Board scores and school grades will mean to him at a particular institution. Except for a rough estimate of his chances of admission, he cannot intelligently inform a child of the risks involved in his ability to do the work at the college of his choice.*

At this point it seems appropriate to turn to what is the most crucial area of educational testing in the United States—the nation's public elementary and high schools. No better introduction can be offered than this

---

*It is to the credit of the American College Testing Program, which serves over 600 colleges, mostly outside the East, that its members will share their own prediction indices with the high schools that desire them.

story related by Professor Lee J. Cronbach, one of the most distinguished authorities in measurement. In the early days of I.Q. testing, he recalled, scores were often interpreted literally, sometimes with ludicrous results. Shortly after the turn of the century a child was brought to America and, as was the custom, took the famous Binet intelligence test. His score was so woefully low that the authorities confined him for a short period to an institution for the mentally deficient. This child who the authorities decided was a mental incompetent eventually became one of the world's most famous statesmen. His name is Jan Masaryk, the late, renowned Czech leader. What no one seemed to realize at the time was that young Masaryk had difficulty understanding the language in which the test was given.

We may begin by asking: With all that has since been learned about the fallibility of mental measurement, do such things happen now?